The Church in the Eternal Purpose of God

The Church in the Eternal Purpose of God

Watchman Nee

Christian Fellowship Publishers, Inc.
New York

ISBN 978-1-937713-40-9

Available from the Publishers at:

11515 Allecingie Parkway
Richmond, Virginia 23235
www.c-f-p.com

Printed in the United States of America

Preface

"My Father worketh even until now, and I work," declared the Lord Jesus while on the earth (John 5:17). Having thus laid the foundation of the work, Christ commands His church to fulfill it in the power of the Holy Spirit. We Christians who are the many-membered body of Christ have a pressing need to know how to serve according to God.

Among this collection of twelve messages delivered by brother Watchman Nee, the first four of them were spoken in English while he was in Europe during the year 1938-39 and appear here in an edited form for the sake of clarity. The remaining eight messages were delivered in Chinese when he was in Kowloon, Hong Kong during the year 1950. Their texts have now been newly translated into English from the original transcriptions in Chinese which were made available to the translator for translation and inclusion in the present volume.

Despite the difference in years when these messages were given, brother Nee's burden was the same: How can we who are members of Christ's church best serve God's purpose?

May God use this compilation to help us to serve His will and purpose more effectively.

Contents

Preface	5
Chapter 1—God's Commitment to the Name	9
Chapter 2—Divine Principles of Service	33
Chapter 3—The Urgent Need of Spiritual Knowledge	59
Chapter 4—One Spirit and One Body	87
Chapter 5—Forsake All to Serve God	117
Chapter 6—Consecration According to Romans 12	129
Chapter 7—Know God's Principle of Work	145
Chapter 8—Spiritual Sense	153
Chapter 9—Spiritual Sense (Concl'd)	167
Chapter 10—How to Make a Decision in the Church	189
Chapter 11—Spiritual Quality	205
Chapter 12—Spiritual Quality (Concl'd)	225

Scripture quotations are from the
American Standard Version of the Bible
(1901), unless otherwise indicated.

Chapter One
God's Commitment to the Name

"Verily I say unto you, What things soever ye shall bind on earth shall be bound in heaven; and what things soever ye shall loose on earth shall be loosed in heaven. Again I say unto you, that if two of you shall agree on earth as touching anything that they shall ask, it shall be done for them of my Father who is in heaven. For where two or three are gathered together in my name, there am I in the midst of them" (Matthew 18:18-20).

"And the seventy returned with joy, saying, Lord, even the demons are subject unto us in thy name" (Luke 10:17).

"And in that day ye shall ask me no question. Verily, verily, I say unto you, if ye shall ask anything of the Father, he will give it you in my name. Hitherto have ye asked nothing in my name: ask, and ye shall receive, that your joy may be made full" (John 16:23-24).

"But Peter said, Silver and gold have I none; but what I have, that give I thee. In the name of Jesus Christ of Nazareth, walk" (Acts 3:6).

"And this she did for many days. But Paul, being sore troubled, turned and said to the spirit, I charge thee in the name of Jesus Christ to come out of her. And it came out that very hour" (Acts 16:18).

> "But certain also of the strolling Jews, exorcists, took upon them to name over them that had the evil spirits the name of the Lord Jesus, saying, I adjure you by Jesus whom Paul preacheth.... And the evil spirit answered and said unto them, Jesus I know, and Paul I know, but who are ye? And the man in whom the evil spirit was leaped on them, and mastered both of them, and prevailed against them, so that they fled out of that house naked and wounded. And this became known to all, both Jews and Greeks, that dwelt at Ephesus; and fear fell upon them all, and the name of the Lord Jesus was magnified" (Acts 19:13, 15-17).

At the outset of our time together today let me say that it is not my purpose that we should go into every detail to be found in the New Testament concerning the name of the Lord Jesus. There is a very wide range of things connected with His name, but that is not what I wish to address. What I feel the Lord would like us to see is that there is the commitment of God to the name of the Lord Jesus. What I have reference to is what can be found in the two passages in Acts 3 and 16 quoted earlier: the first involving Peter with a crippled man and the second involving Paul with a girl possessed with an evil spirit.

The crippled man asked for money, but Peter's response was: "Silver and gold I have none, but what I have I give to you; in the name of Jesus Christ of Nazareth, walk." The point is this: Peter did not kneel down and pray first; he did not, so to speak, ask for the mind of the Lord first; he did not say to the man, "Now here you are, a lame man, who needs healing; but I do not know whether it is the Lord's will to heal you or not; so you wait here and let me go and pray, and if the case is worse, I will fast for a day or so and then I will come back and say what is the mind of the Lord concerning your case." No, Peter did not do anything of the sort. There was no question of seeking to know the mind or will of God at all. Later we shall see what all this means, but the point is, Peter did not stop to immediately do anything of that kind; rather, he instantly said, Walk, in the name of the Lord Jesus.

Then the same thing happened with Paul involving that slave girl possessed by an evil spirit. There was no approach made by Paul to God concerning His will or mind; he simply took cognizance of the situation and commanded the spirit to depart in the name of the Lord Jesus, and the deliverance was accomplished immediately; that very hour the spirit left her. So what does this conduct by these two apostles indicate? Why is there no seeking before the Lord, no requesting to know His mind before action is taken? This is what we are going to attempt to understand, and it has to do with the commitment of God.

How We Should Work for the Lord

Here we are considering how we should work for the Lord. No work is worthy of the designation—"the work of God"—if God is not willing to commit himself to such work. Whenever God is in support of something, He will commit himself to it. I cannot say that I am working, doing, or attempting something for God if He has not yet committed himself to it. In the Scriptures we shall find that this principle is fully summed up in the phrase: in His name!—meaning that neither Paul nor Peter, in their service for God, did anything out from themselves. They both commanded: In His name! What, then, does this mean? It means that a person cannot take someone's name and use it unless that name has been committed to me by that someone.

A brother recently asked me to write a letter that would say that I have received from him something, but without my knowing what it is he would be giving to me. He merely said, You must trust me; at the letter's beginning simply write "Received" and then sign at the letter's bottom, and let me put in between what you have received. So, I trusted him and I signed. He could thus use my name, for I had committed myself to this undertaking.

Now in order to be a real servant of the Lord we must be able to use His name as though it were our own name, and that such authorization from the Lord is His commitment. If God has committed himself to whatever He has called me to do, I can use His name—so to speak—quite freely. There is a condition laid down for that to occur (and this will be discussed shortly), but the point to be brought out here is that if you cannot obtain God's commitment of himself to what you are doing—may I humbly say this?—then I doubt very much that your work is possessed of any spiritual value. We must be able to stand up and say with confidence, In the name!

The securing of such commitment is not a matter which I must engage in at the moment when things are happening. The whole matter has been settled between God himself and me His servant long before this present moment. Heretofore I had become so one with the Lord—so committed to Him—and have continued to be in such union and identification with Him that I can use His name and He will back it up. Command the lame to walk, and He will back it up; command the demon to go, and He will stand behind what I say. Such is the authority which the servant of God is able to wield in faith.

Has God Committed Himself to the Work?

During these years of my little service for the Lord in China I have always tried to determine one thing: Am I able to stand up and do a given work and know that God will never deny that He has committed himself, that He has decreed that it is indeed His work? That truth—that reality—must be settled first. Once that is settled one can always use His name quite freely. Two or three may be gathered together in agreement, and they thus can bind something on earth in the Lord's name, and the thing will be bound in heaven. God in heaven has to recognize the act on earth.

It is not that as something is happening I must try to determine at that very moment what the mind of the Lord is concerning it. Because I am in such union and identification with Him, whatever work for the Lord is required at that moment can be done immediately. My union with God in Christ has hitherto already been formed, and that is thus a present fact. All the flesh, all that is of the natural, all soulish life in me must be dealt with, because my union with the Lord is such that He has something down here which He cannot deny up there. Because of that present fact I can move as a real representative of Him. When I use the Lord's name He will not deny it. If I set anything free here on earth He will set it free in heaven; if I bind it here He must have it bound there.

The union established must be such that at the time of need we have not to try to lay hold of God, but, facing the demand of the moment either before God or before Satan, we can use His name freely and Satan has to acknowledge, "Jesus I know, and Paul I know ..." Praise God for the second name, "Paul I know." If hell only knows *Jesus* then we are helpless, but praise the Lord, hell knows the Son of God and at the same time knows those who are in true union and identification with the Son. That tells us a great deal about Hades. "Jesus I know, and Paul I know, but who are you?" That is a most telling question. Those who do not know the Lord, and those who are not in union with Him, will be taken no account of by demons. The whole point is, are we in such a union with the Lord that God has most assuredly to commit himself to what we are doing?

I do not know what you have been doing for the Lord, and I do not know what kind of work God has been calling you to do. Many a time you will find that you have to attempt work with only the promises of God at your back with no natural help whatever before you. And if you take that course, will God come in and back you and the work up, or will He recant? What is necessary is that we must be on such terms with God that whatever we do, whatever service we are engaged in, God cannot deny that He has sent us and that He has a part in it.

So the real secret of divine service is always to secure God's commitment, so to speak, to our work. Once we have that, all hell may break forth attempting to stop it, accompanied by suffering, testing and trouble; yet, you can simply smile knowing that you are coming successfully to the other side. In this connection, I remember once I was talking to someone who commented as follows: If I had the word of the Lord to go to the other side of the lake, and if I were on a boat taking me there, and there arose a storm which fiercely raged, and the Lord was sleeping in the stern of the boat, then I would sit at the very head of the boat and look out upon the troubling waves and smile, and cry out: Come on! Come up high! Come up higher! Try to see what you can do! I would even laugh at the wind and the waves; for has not the Lord committed himself?

Let me say that if the Lord has indeed committed himself, then you can have the attitude of faith, believing that you will be carried through to the other side of whatever the situation may be. Without *that*, however, you cannot even begin.

Practical Steps to God's Commitment

We want to move on to more practical issues—for example, the necessity to find out how one can work in such a way that God has to commit himself. How must I work that I shall have the full commitment of God behind me? We will briefly consider several points here, even though some of this presentation may be covering old ground; nevertheless, I hope that those who are familiar with such ground will bear with me, because we all should acknowledge that whatever is truly spiritual can never grow old.

1. Revelation of God's Eternal Purpose

I believe the first essential we must have as workers for God is a true revelation of His eternal purpose. I cannot envision anyone having an effective work for God without knowing what is His eternal will and mind. If, for example, I do not know that the architect of my employer is intent on building a house, or a garage, or an aerodrome, how can I possibly be of help? I must know the purpose or plan behind the work of construction—though I may not have any part in drawing up the plan—in order for me to be a good laborer in connection with it. I must know what the architect or builder is after, and even though my part may be a very small one; indeed, it may be that I am nothing more than a bearer of bricks or of mortar or of cement: that is, nothing but a common laborer. Yet, however small my part is going to be in that plan or work, I must at least know what that plan, aim or purpose is that the builder or architect is after.

I am sorry to have to say that at the present time evangelism has come to be embraced as *the* work for God. Now I believe fully in the necessity of preaching God's word and that God is very much active in sending out the gospel and bringing people in; but gospel preaching should not and cannot be an unrelated activity. It is truly related to God's eternal purpose and has a place therein, but only has *a* place therein. For I must here declare that if gospel preaching is viewed as the center and sum in God's scheme of things, then that worker for God has not discerned or known God's eternal purpose at all.

Let us who serve God realize that real gospel preaching and soul-winning is but a means to an end, it is not the end in itself. God's end and purpose is His Son. All the redeemed sons whom God shall ultimately bring in will be brought into the kingdom in order that the Son may have the preeminence in all things (Colossians 1:18b), that the Son may have that central position which the Father had ordained for Him from the very beginning. God has always wanted to glorify His Son—to crown Him with honor and glory. All the redeemed children who will have been brought in are only for the Son. If we see and acknowledge *that*, then we know the eternal purpose of God.

The essential point is this: that we must continually have in view the eternal purpose of God. If I mistake not, we are living in the end-period of the church age, and I do believe that many of God's people today think the same. And if that be true, then what should be our specific part in relation to that eternal purpose? Everyone in his or her generation has a particular relationship to God's purpose. Our generation being at the very end of this age, however, there is, so to speak, a slight difference as to our relationship to that plan and purpose of His. And what accounts for that difference? It is simply this: that, today, the eyes of God are turning towards the matter of the kingdom, in that the age of the church is in the process of being brought to an end so that the kingdom can be brought in. Organized Christianity is going to be set aside whereas the sovereignty of the Lord Jesus is going to be established on the earth. If I am not greatly mistaken, this is what is immediately before us. Indeed, this is what God is after today: His desire that the kingdom be brought in.

We know that in Scripture Solomon serves as a type of the Lord Jesus as the King in the kingdom of God, and we also know that, by contrast, David serves as another type of the Lord Jesus—in this case, as the Warrior who will bring in the kingdom. In other words, David represents the warring side of the Lord for the purpose of bringing in the kingdom whereas Solomon symbolizes the Lord's reigning side for the purpose of ruling over the kingdom; and hence, today the call to each of us is, I will be a warrior standing with David to bring in the kingdom so that the Lord Jesus can be Solomon who will reign over it. The trouble with many believers in our day is that they are not warring; they do not possess that necessary fighting spirit. They apparently have not seen that the kingdom can only be brought in by spiritual warfare: that is to say, by the kind of prayer warfare which can bring in the kingdom so that the Lord Jesus could reign and exercise His God-ordained sovereignty over the whole earth.

Now in the light of the aforesaid purpose of God in desiring to have the kingdom brought in, I wish you to please excuse me for asking a very bold and frank question of you who have been serving God by endeavoring to win souls to the Lord either in this land or in foreign lands: In all your evangelistic labors for God, what have you been doing in relation to His purpose of bringing in the kingdom? Yes, you may have been doing a hundred and one very good and precious things for God, but with respect to the bringing in of His kingdom at this time, what have you been doing as to *that*? For that is what God is seeking after today.

God is seeking to have some souls here and there who will be instruments to bring in the kingdom. But for that to occur, the first issue every true worker for God must have settled is the identification of that worker's purpose with the purpose of God. If God is after that, then I as His servant will pursue after that: if that is what He is after, then I will do everything to reach that end.

This means that I must have the enlarged objective ever in view. None of us who have been called to teach or instruct can really present the whole matter before you; rather, this whole matter must come to you with such revelational power and grip you in such a way that you will deem every other work to be secondary. Such spiritual priority is what God is after for such a time as this. When the eyes of your heart have been opened, you will see what, at the end of this age, God is truly after. Then it will be quite easy for you and me to find our personal sphere of ministry.

The trouble today with so many Christians is that they do not know the "capital W" will of God, and instead, they try to discern the various "small w" wills of God. They attempt to seek out what is the will of God for them today as to this, that, and the other, but it is all unrelated and fragmentary. We cannot obtain and place the will of God in its right perspective by such means as that. We have to see the eternal will, what God has been seeking after and working towards throughout the ages. True, the small detail guidance can easily be fitted into the much greater one, but the latter must be made known to us first—and that by revelation. It is something too vast for our human minds to grasp in its totality; nevertheless, praise God, it *can* be known; and some of us must confess that we have caught glimpses of it, that we have seen something of God's eternal purpose; and we have come to realize that it is something which, when it is known, settles all the small questions or details of guidance.

2. A Personal Knowledge of God's Mind

I would now draw our attention to a very practical aspect in our discussion on God's eternal purpose. I take it for granted that we have now all seen His eternal will.

What, therefore, are we going to do concerning our work? God's eternal purpose is so immense, and when I turn my attention back to my own sphere of work, what am I to do? Hence, I come to the second point in our discussion today. All true service for God can only be initiated on the basis of one's personal knowledge of His mind. No man in and of himself can conceive anything for God, and then ask God to bless it and call it His own. If a work is going to be spiritually effective and possess some spiritual value to God, that work must be utterly from Him himself. God must be the one who has conceived it and initiated it.

The trouble with so many so-called Christian workers today is that man has initiated a work and has then asked God to bless it. But let us realize that God will never commit himself to that. Yet, in stating this I do not mean to be saying there will be no blessing whatever. In fact, many a time God does condescend to bless a bit of work here and a bit of work there, but one should never expect God to commit himself to that work. A Christian worker should never say with respect to his own initiated work: In His name! Instead, he can only legitimately use his own name. God has never agreed that such a worker should use His name in that way.

Even the Lord Jesus acknowledged that "the Son can do nothing of [or: by, out of] himself" (John 5:19a). Thus meaning that the Lord Jesus has never initiated any work in and of himself. Every true spiritual work must be started by God. His will is the beginning of divine service. We must come to the point where we decide that if God does not move, we will not move—that if the Lord does not start anything, say anything, go anywhere, then I will refuse to do it.

We read in the book of Acts of how the Spirit forbids and permits not. How ironic that these forbiddances to initiate actions are mentioned in the book of *Acts*. We would think that these should be mentioned in "the book of Inactivities or of Inactions." Too often we think that the actual doing of something is serving God. Yet many a time if we would *refrain* from doing things, God would gain far more glory. It is only when we have learned the lesson of *not* doing that God will use us to do. Similarly, if we cannot keep quiet for Him, He can never send us to speak for Him. Oh, the divine necessity for God to be the one to initiate some activity and of our remaining quiet. If that spiritual understanding be known, I believe that man would have no place: we would realize that for any undertaking for God to be spiritual it must be utterly out from God in its origination.

So we have thus far addressed two very essential issues here. The first is the necessity of our having a revelation of the divine eternal purpose; the second is the need for our having a knowledge of God's will in respect of my specific sphere of work. Without these essentials being true of us, God will not commit himself.

3. Work Must Be Done by God's Power

But having those two essentials does not effect a spiritual conclusion to the work. True, the work ought to flow out of God’s will; but how should the work be carried forth and executed? Answer: In its beginning, God!—and in its continuance, the power of God! The will of God is to be the beginning of our specific work for Him; the power of God is to be the continuance of our work for Him.

Mankind has been talking about power for centuries, and in many a book you can buy today you can more or less read about the issue of power. Or whenever you might hear someone giving an address, the critique given at the end is that he is either a very powerful speaker or that he has no power at all. The matter of power looms very large on our horizon. What is power, after all? Many a time I have heard a brother coming back from a meeting saying, Oh, the preacher tonight had power! In response I would always put forth this comment and question: Yes, no doubt he had power, but can you tell me what power he had? It is not a question of his having power, but what power was it?

So we have before us a question as to the nature of the power employed in service for God. If God is not the initiator of the work, then He will not commit himself to it. And even if God did initiate the work but the Christian worker was using his own power to accomplish divine ends, God would still not commit himself to that work. The simple fact is that God’s will must govern the beginning of the work and His power must govern the ongoing process of the work because He will never utilize human power to accomplish His will.

I can assure you that some of us have gone through deep waters to learn that one single lesson. God will not use whatever there is of me to get His will done. That has to be put away. And hence, there comes to the fore the issue of the soul verses the spirit; there comes into view the place of our natural energy; there arises the question of the power of the flesh.

It is well known that there is a kind of person in society who has great managing powers. Such a person knows how to do and manage things in a very good way but at the same time he may be a very poor speaker. There are others who may be good preachers but are very poor managers: if various affairs are placed into their hands they cannot manage the situation as well as they can preach.

In my service for the Lord in China I try to determine how brethren are actually going on with the Lord. Many a time I find a brother who is a good business manager, and I say to him, Brother, we have a very important task needing to be done; I wonder whether you would be kind enough to help us out on this! That brother will be most willing and very confident, he feeling quite sufficient in being able to do it; for he will say, Oh, yes, I think I can do that because it is not a difficult task. On the other hand, were I to ask this same brother if he would like to give a word next Lord's day morning, he would reply, No, I do not think I am the man to do that; indeed, I don't think I am able to do that.

Now if I were to ask this same brother to undertake a task along business lines, how hard do you think he would pray for divine help? I do not think he would pray very hard, for he would think himself to be quite up to handling the matter. If I were to tell him, though, that next week we feel he must come and give us a message, how hard would he pray? I believe he would pray far harder over that endeavor than over the business task. Why do I say that? It is because that brother would most likely say to himself, I cannot preach this message myself, I must cast myself on God. In other words, he feels quite sufficient only for what he feels he can do in and of himself. This is what is known as natural energy in its simplest form. What, therefore, is natural energy? It is the power a person can exercise naturally without the need for divine help.

The trouble with us all is just this: There are many works we can do without relying upon God, there are many services we can fulfill without depending upon God, there are many undertakings we dare to attempt without the slightest reliance upon God—and all because we know we can. That is an accurate picture of the natural energy of man. That is human—not divine—power. It is that which is born of the flesh and which will continue to remain flesh. And hence, this natural energy in us has to be dealt with. We must be brought to the point of even being afraid of doing anything, to the point of knowing that we are not sufficient in ourselves to undertake doing any work for God.

Let us recall two particular words, one to be found in Acts and the other to be found in Exodus, both of which are concerned with Moses. You will remember that Stephen told his hearers that Moses was a man of deeds and of words (see Acts 7:22b). Mind you, that observation is most important to bear in mind. Moses was described by Stephen as being a man of words and powerful in speech. But then we learn from Exodus that after Moses had been dealt with by God for many years in the wilderness, what did Moses say concerning himself? "I am not a man of words; rather, I am slow of speech and have a slow tongue"! (Exodus 4:10 mgn) And so, God had to appoint Moses' brother Aaron to be his mouthpiece, to speak for him (vv.14-16). When the heretofore orator came to a point in his life wherein he could no longer speak well, then it can be said that this man has had his natural energy dealt with.

Like Moses we need the hand of God to come upon us granting us light and revelation in showing us that whatever we are naturally able to do is that which is only out from ourselves and is therefore something which we cannot and must not do because such work or service is unacceptable to God since it is not His will. Consequently, whenever that natural ability of ours has been touched and dealt with—that is to say, whenever such a necessary lesson has been truly learned—then the result will be that like Moses we shall recoil from undertaking any activity which is out from ourselves.

Such an experience stands as a crisis in our Christian walk. Each one of us must one day be brought before God to be dealt with as to our natural energy. Even so, when that has been successfully dealt with, each of us shall find the circle of God's dealing will be widened even further; but there must first be that fundamental dealing of God with our natural life. I do not know how much natural energy there is in the so-called work of God today among God's people! But I know that there are many labors for God for which we barely, if at all, need to rely upon divine power for their accomplishment; that there are many so-called spiritual works over which we need not pray; that with respect to many tasks presumably undertaken by us for the Lord we believe we need not lay ourselves aside but we can simply take up and perform because we in ourselves are quite able to do. But the Lord has told us this: "Apart from me ye can do nothing" (John 15:5c).

Whatever we have done in serving God which has been undertaken apart from relying upon and taking power from the Lord is nothing. The Lord has declared that such labor is nothing, and that it will always remain as nothing. It may be great piles of work that we have done, but if not done according to God's power, it will be deemed by Him to be wood, hay, and stubble (I Corinthians 3:12). Wood is that which is the result of man's effort; hay is dried grass and represents the dead glory of man; and stubble is symbolic of dried-up human nature. All these efforts from man are nothing according to God's estimation. Divine work can never be done without divine energy that is of God and not of us. We must rely upon Him, lay hold of Him, and appropriate Him. We have to arrive at the point in our walk and work for God when we say, God, I have got nothing and therefore I in myself cannot do it. And as we humbly acknowledge this, we shall discover that God is doing it. Praise God, whenever we cease from our own works, He begins to do His. Hence, it comes down to this: What kind of power am I using?

I remember one day a brother commented to me as follows: I have observed a number of Christians who were very useful to the Lord, doing many works, but then they accepted the teaching that they must conform to the death of Christ and take up the cross in dealing with their natural life; and consequently, they have ended up doing nothing for God. I don't think, he added, that that teaching is practical at all, because such Christians had heretofore been most useful in performing much labor for the Lord but after embracing the teaching of the cross in relation to the natural man, they simply became useless in God's service.

My response was: Brother, let me inquire as to what those Christian works were, after all? What had they been doing prior to accepting the teaching? If their work was altogether out from themselves in terms of men's natural energy, then I can tell you that when those works go through death nothing of worth to God will come forth onto the other side of death simply because the cross slays everything of the natural. If it is altogether of natural power or human thought, no one should wonder that nothing of that kind will go through death and be able to come forth onto resurrection ground. On the other hand, if in the natural life of those Christians there is that which has its origin in God and is subjected to the process of the death of the Lord, then they will learn that though whatever is of the natural man will be slain, whatever is of God can never be slain by the cross. Indeed, such an outcome is impossible; on the contrary, whatever has its origin in God will always come through death onto resurrection ground most gloriously.

So the essential point here is this: Does the Christian worker possess anything which is of God or only from the natural? Is all one's work and labors out from one's self? In fact, are you the one who is doing the work? If so, you will ultimately realize that when brought through the cross, nothing of such work can or will survive.

The cross today and the fire in the days to come will have been accomplishing the same result. Whatever can withstand the cross today will always be able to withstand the fire in the future time. Resurrection life signifies that which is unshakable, that which is eternal, that which even the cross cannot slay; rather, it will always come forth in resurrection glory.

Hence, one simple revelatory test is this (and here I must add that I do not want you to be introspective; nevertheless, this is a very good test): If you would like to know what kind of power you possess for doing the work of God, simply apply this test: If you bring that work to death, can it still come forth—can it survive? That will settle the entire matter. If you are not relying upon yourself and refuse anything which you in yourself can do, you will discern how much remains of the work; and by this means you will know how much there is of the Lord in the work. I have always found in the work of God that He invariably asks me to do that which I myself can never do, and I have always done that which I could not do. Similarly, in our daily life here on earth, God never asks us to live a life *we* are able to live. In both circumstances, our resource is from God, our power is of Him; and hence, we must refuse everything that is of man. Oh Lord, deal with me!

4. The End of God's Work: His Glory

As was indicated earlier, the starting point is the will of God and the process is the power of God. But I want now for us to consider more closely that the end of the work of God is His glory. His will begins everything, His power accomplishes everything, and His glory fills everything. The end of all divine work is therefore the glory of God and not my pleasure nor my enjoyment. If our desire and focus is upon service *to the Lord* and not upon our enjoyment, the happier we are and the less condemnation there will be in our hearts. The more glory we seek for ourselves the more condemnation we shall have in our consciousness.

Permit me to make an observation here which some of us know quite well. When you have truly learned the secret of allowing the cross to deal with the natural man, you come to realize that, in doing a work for God which He has indeed commanded you to do, you obey and do the work, yet not because you necessarily like it. In fact, you may feel it to be death in doing that particular work; but because you have been brought to the place of having such a knowledge of the Lord and of invoking such a refusal of yourself, you find that even death is good.

For example, it is not because I feel happy preaching, therefore I will preach; it is not because I feel that in doing such a work I shall obtain much emotional enjoyment out of it, therefore I will follow through with it; nor is it because I sense that I will be a hero if I carry through with the task God has commanded me to do. No, it is to be nothing for myself! The only thing which fills my eyes is the glory which God will receive as a result of my doing the work. My concern shall only be: How can I glorify God in this undertaking? Whether I like it or dislike it, that is not the point nor does it matter; I do it because of Him. He receives all the glory by my accomplishing the work and I gain nothing out of it. As a matter of fact, the more you and I stay out of it the better, and God obtains the more glory.

If and when the aforementioned issues are settled in a Christian worker's ministry for the Lord, I can assure you of this very truth: that God must indeed commit himself to that servant's work; the latter can use God's name as though it were that of God's servant. There will be no danger now. Yet, having said that, I do not mean that we can be idle and unwatchful; but the point is, there must be such an utter identification of ourselves with the interests of God alone and the utter refusal and denial of ourselves. When anyone has arrived at that point, he will realize that he can use the name of the Lord to accomplish any task, and furthermore, all hell must recognize his authority.

I have to confess that many a time we in China have come face to face with very difficult situations, more difficult than some of us could have imagined; but as we came to the place of utter identification with the Lord and His interests we were able to use His name as though it were our own, and praise God, the Lord has stood in support of it. He did not deny our authority in using the name.

We must all learn to come to that place in our Christian walk wherein whatever undertaking we assume for God shall be backed up by His commitment to the name of the Lord which we wield as though it were our own in dealing with this or that challenging situation. And if we do arrive at that place, we shall see that the approach to the Father with the name of the Lord works and that the approach to the demons with the name of the Lord likewise works; that whatever is bound down here on earth will be bound in heaven and that whatever is loosed down here will be loosed in heaven. All our work which is of God will thus have His commitment and His backing.

CHAPTER TWO
DIVINE PRINCIPLES OF SERVICE

"Speak unto the children of Israel, and take of them rods, one for each fathers' house, of all their princes according to their fathers' houses, twelve rods: write thou every man's name upon his rod. And thou shalt write Aaron's name upon the rod of Levi; for there shall be one rod for each head of their fathers' houses. And thou shalt lay them up in the tent of meeting before the testimony, where I meet with you. And it shall come to pass, that the rod of the man whom I shall choose shall bud: and I will make to cease from me the murmurings of the children of Israel, which they murmur against you" (Numbers 17:2-5).

"And Jesus when he was baptized, went up straightway from the water: and lo, the heavens were opened unto him, and he saw the Spirit of God descending as a dove, and coming upon him; and lo, a voice out of the heavens, saying, This is my beloved Son, in whom I am well pleased" (Matthew 3:16-17).

"And behold, I send forth the promise of my Father upon you: but tarry ye in the city, until ye be clothed with power from on high" (Luke 24:49).

We today wish to consider the divine principles to be observed in our service to God. There are specific principles which no one who is intent on serving God can deviate from. The principles which God has laid down in His word for service to Him are as definite and specific as the conditions or principles for salvation. We cannot change the conditions for salvation; on the contrary, no one can ever obtain salvation that way. Similarly, we cannot change the conditions for service to God. If change is sought, no one will ever be used by God.

The primary condition or basis for salvation rests upon Jesus' death and resurrection and upon no other ground and is thus the ground or basis for our acceptance to God. Likewise, the principle of the death and resurrection of the Lord is the primary condition or basis for our service to God. Our salvation rests on the fact of the death and on the fact of the resurrection of the Lord Jesus, and our service to God is based on the principle of death—yet not exactly on the fact of death itself but the principle of death, nevertheless—and on the principle of the resurrection of the Lord.

The Principles of Jesus' Death and Resurrection

By God's grace we today want to see and understand a little how the principle of the death and the principle of the resurrection of the Lord Jesus govern our service to Him. No one can be a true servant of God without knowing these two principles. Even Jesus himself served on that ground. You learn from Matthew 3 that before His public ministry ever began Jesus experienced water baptism. He was baptized even though He had no sin or fault which needed to be repented of and cleansed. Now we know the symbolic meaning of baptism is death and resurrection. And hence, Jesus' ministry could not begin until He came onto that ground himself. It was only after He had assumed the ground of being dead and resurrected as symbolized by His being baptized that He then served, that He then ministered.

Let us take note of what happened at the Lord's baptism. As He came up out of the water of baptism, the Holy Spirit came down and rested upon Him on the basis of His forthcoming death and resurrection, and then He ministered. So we can safely say this, that all the work which the Lord accomplished on earth prior to His actual death and resurrection was done on the basis of death and resurrection, even though the actual Calvary experience and the actual resurrection experience still awaited Him in the future. It was on the ground of what Jesus' baptism signified—namely, His death and resurrection—that He served the Father.

Now if the Son of man had to go through death and resurrection in order to serve and work, then no servant of God today can serve Him at all without actually knowing in experience these two principles of death and resurrection. Jesus made this very clear to His discipled servants when He ascended back to the Father. By that time He had died and had been resurrected, and so He told them to wait in Jerusalem for the Spirit to come upon them as well.

Now what is this Spirit, this "power from on high" (Luke 24:49b, Acts 1:4b)? The Spirit of power from on high which those first disciples were waiting for was nothing less than the virtue of the death and resurrection of the Lord Jesus. To put it another way, the Holy Spirit is the vessel, so to speak, into which the death and resurrection of the Lord has been deposited. He is the One who contains that virtue of the Lord Jesus. That explains why the Holy Spirit could only be given after the Lord Jesus had been glorified. So it is only when this Spirit—this power from on high—rests upon men and women that they can witness and serve in other ways. Without the experience of death and without the experience of resurrection as the basis of our service to God, there is no testimony possible, and there can be no true servants for God.

If we turn to the Old Testament we shall find the same principle is there. We have read together a very familiar passage from Numbers 17. Back then the matter of Aaron's ministry had been contested, great doubt and suspicion having been expressed as to whether Aaron was truly called of God as a minister to Him and His people. The Israelites had wondered aloud: Whether Aaron has been ordained of God or not, we do not know! Accordingly, God set about establishing beyond any doubt who was His true servant and who was not.

How did Jehovah God do this? Twelve dead rods—one for each tribe of Israel, with Aaron's name written on the rod of Levi—were to be placed before Him in the tabernacle over against the testimony, and they were to be there for a night. And God declared that the rod which budded and blossomed and brought forth fruit was the man chosen by Him to be minister. We all know the meaning of this event: the budding rod speaks of resurrection, and thus death and resurrection is the basis of true God-recognized ministry. Aaron's dead but then budded-and-blossomed-and-fruitful rod proved that his ministry was truly God-recognized. God will only recognize us as His ministers if we have truly gone through a death-and-resurrection experience. No one can serve the Lord without his having come onto resurrection ground.

What It Means to Go through Death and Resurrection

I wish to come back a few minutes later to this subject of the budding rod and the principle for our work with the Lord which it represents. For now, however, I want us to consider together some practical aspects associated with that principle. For it is very easy to receive a truth as a principle and admire it, and yet lose out in its implementation in one's personal life. To have admiration in our hearts for the truth of it is one thing, but to be blessed by it is quite another. Hence, I would like for us to focus for a few minutes on some of the practical implications inherent in experiencing this vital spiritual principle in order that we may see what it means practically for the believer to go through death and resurrection in his or her spiritual life.

1. & 2. Jesus' Death Works on Both Sins and Sin

We are aware of how the death of Jesus has done its work with respect to the matter of sins; I refer, of course, to the issue of man's forgiveness. We who are saved realize that our forgiveness is based on Jesus' shed blood: if there is no blood shed there can be no remission or forgiveness of sins (Matthew 26:28, Hebrews 9:22). We see, therefore, that the death of Christ has its effectiveness with regard to sins.

At this point I believe that Romans 6 quite naturally comes into view; for we know that our old man has been crucified. Yet to what end? To what purpose? It is that we do not serve sin. So what is brought into view here is not sins but sin and its power. Many of us, I trust, have seen that reality. At some point in your life God opened your eyes to see that your old man has been crucified, and in reaction you most likely shouted for joy and praised the Lord that the terrible old man whom you tried to deal with for years and had failed has now been dealt with on the cross of Christ, and henceforth sin will never oppress. And such is the blessed effect of the death of the Lord Jesus with respect to the matter of sin in its power and operation in us, and that is most precious.

Yes, we do not want to underestimate the vital importance of that aspect of Calvary's death, but even that does not touch the core of the subject which we are going to consider next. Indeed, we must begin our walk on the pathway towards God-recognized service by experiencing death, for death to sin is the initial step which leads us into our true service to God; yet even that does not make us a true God-recognized servant. We bless God for Romans 6 which points up how the power of sin has been destroyed because the old man has been dealt with; but that does not yet touch the central issue.

3. Jesus' Death Also Works on Yielding Up Our Will

Let us realize that when once the issue surrounding the power of sin has been settled, thus enabling us to reckon what has happened to us in the Lord, then the matter of yielding to God's will makes its appearance; by which is meant that the issue of self-will, the dealing with our human will, comes into view; for certainly the place of consecration or surrender or yielding comes into play, because in its working death operates in such a way that I am willing to let go my will and am now willing to obey the Lord.

Praise God, Romans 6 has most assuredly been a real blessing, and we praise Him with all our hearts for our yielding that day when we came to God and said, Yes!, and bade goodbye forever to our sins. We praise God as well for that day when we came to Him and allowed the Lord's death to deal with our wills. Jesus' death not only works upon our sins and sin but likewise upon our self-will. And in one sense that constitutes our ministry; yet even in our experience of these operations of Jesus' death on us, the core of the matter has nonetheless not been touched.

This third realm—that of our self-will—on which the death of the Lord Jesus has done its necessary work still does not constitute the end of that death's vital work. I do not mean to say, however, that it is not precious, because it was unquestionably a red-letter day for us all when we moved over to God's side and refused to live according to ourselves. Nevertheless, there are many genuinely consecrated saints who do not know what is their natural life by which they too often live. Doubtless there is consecration in their lives, there may unquestionably even be surrender and the yielding up of their will, but there is nonetheless a lack of the knowledge of what is meant by the soul and the natural energy which animates it. And this is what I shall address later on.

4. Jesus' Death Works on the Holiness of Our Life

Then there is a fourth aspect or realm which is quite popular and known to many of God's saints. This particular aspect is presented in Romans 7. In that chapter it is not the subject of sins nor that of sin nor that of the will which is in view, but it is the matter of the holiness of life which is in view.

Romans 7 relates the struggle of a true man of God who was trying to please Him in walking in righteousness. The entire topic of discussion in this chapter revolves around the subject not of service but of living out a life of personal holiness; that is to say, the narrator greatly desires to live a holy and righteous life for God! But the author of Romans 7 had it all wrong. What had Paul been doing which made it impossible for him to achieve that goal? Simply put, he was constantly bringing himself under the power of law and not grace; which meant that he was attempting to be obedient to God's holy standard of life by his natural power.

Now mark you, there is a great difference between the power spoken of in Romans 7—the power of the law—and the power which I am going to speak of, which is the natural human power of man. I believe, of course, that there is a link between the two; nonetheless, there is a distinction to be made between these two powers. Now in Romans 7 we observe a man of God who for the most part does not have in mind for his consideration the subject of ministry to God. Instead, the whole issue confronting him is the necessity of obeying the law of God. The law made demands upon him of either doing or desiring certain things or refraining from doing or desiring certain other things. And so he tried to live up to those demands of God's law by his own power, which power he vigorously exercised in order to please God in his daily living, but he failed again and again. From this we realize that the cross has to come upon this fourth aspect or realm also; in other words, Jesus' death has to deal with us in this realm as well so that we are brought eventually to the point of declaring: I in myself cannot please God, so I will not any longer attempt to do so.

Please do not misunderstand me here. Yes, the cross does have to bring each of us to that point wherein we must each confess: I in myself cannot do anything, therefore I will not try to do anything; I in myself cannot please God in living according to holiness and righteousness; therefore, from henceforth I am not even going to attempt to please God. But that does not mean that from now on you will never please God. On the contrary, you *shall* please Him, yet not any longer by means of your natural power. Hereafter your heart attitude will be one in which you sincerely declare: I cannot and will not for I know it will be utter futility to try to obey God with my power in order to measure up to His standard of holiness for living. Consequently, it is necessary for Jesus' death to cut down and negate my natural power in trying to please God in my life. In my heart I refuse to involve myself with any of that; rather, I shall only trust the Holy Spirit to bring out God's standard in me, for I am not able in myself to produce that for God; I must trust God to produce His standard of life in me.

I believe some of us have passed through deep waters to realize this in our spiritual life. Perhaps each one has gone through much trying and trying and ever trying again to achieve a victorious resolution to the matter yet without success; but finally coming to the realization of the futility of it all; and only then arriving at the point at which we have had to acknowledge: Oh God, I cannot in myself measure up to Your standard of living; I cannot obey Your law of holiness and righteousness; I can only trust You to bring all that out in me. Only when this realization has been arrived at and is sincerely acknowledged and confessed can it be said that Jesus' death is now in operation upon anyone who seeks to serve God.

5. Jesus' Death Works on Our Natural Strength and Energy

Yet, with all these workings of Jesus' death having been experienced in a believer's life, one is nevertheless left with an incomplete experience of the principle of the Lord's death. This is because there is one remaining realm or sphere which Jesus' death must work upon if we are going to be of use to God; otherwise, it will still be unsafe for Him to use us. As we Chinese might phrase the matter, How many of God's servants are used by the Lord to build twelve feet, but they then try to pull down fifteen feet! In other words, you presumably are being used but at the same time you are destroying your own work because of there being an area in your life which has remained undealt with. Now it is the particular undealt-with area which I had alluded to a few minutes ago that I wish for us to consider together at this time. And it is my prayer that God will grant us grace to see and understand what it is which must be dealt with. Now the undealt-with realm or aspect to which I made reference earlier has to do with the matter of our soul and its natural energy. Please bear in mind, though, that this soulish energy I now have in mind is quite different from what I have previously mentioned. Let me say here that all the many dealings by Jesus' death which we have already discussed and which we may have experienced does not cause us to truly know and experience the working of the principle of the Lord's death upon our soul's natural energy. So let us not mix these things up. I do not wish to go into a lot of analysis; nevertheless, we need to maintain the distinction. Soul energy in relation to our service for God is quite different from those other realms or aspects of our lives that we have mentioned which have needed to be dealt with by Jesus' death.

Before proceeding any further, permit me to speak personally. I do not know what your experience has been nor how you have coped with this issue of the soul, but I must speak for myself, in that I have found this to be one of the costliest areas of life to delve into; and I must confess that it is one of the most difficult things to realize because a person is so very easily deceived even by himself in this respect. Moreover, when one has gained just a little initial experience, one could easily pretend to have gained the whole experience and to assume that one knows more than one actually does. Hence, I would like that by God's grace we tread slowly in our attempt to learn how we should deal with this challenging subject of the soul's energy.

First of all, let us inquire as to what this soul power or natural energy is of which we speak. In its simplest terms—and here I wish to avoid becoming too technical—the natural energy or power of the soul is that which enables you to do, that power which you have from nature. This soulish power is present with us all. Those who have been taught by God repudiate it as a life-animating principle. They refuse to live and serve God by it. They will not let such power reign over their lives nor will they allow it to be the power-spring of the work of God. On the other hand, those who have not been taught of God rely upon it and utilize it, they assuming that it is the power by which they are to serve God.

Let me illustrate this latter situation by taking my mind as an example. I had a keen mind before conversion: and thus in those two words, keen mind, we have a definition, in part, of what the power or natural energy of the soul is. So what is natural energy? Natural energy is that which a person has, apart from new birth. Before experiencing spiritual new birth a person had mental energy quite naturally. It is therefore what comes with, and is developed from, one's natural or physical birth, and is being exercised as a kind of capability to produce or do things in one's natural life. And such ability constitutes, in part, what the natural energy of the soul is.

But, then, a person meets the Savior and experiences the new birth in Christ: for those of us who believe and are converted, a deep work of God has been effected in our spirits: He has now become "the Father of our spirits" (Hebrews 12:9b mgn) and an essential union with Him in Christ has been effected there. Just here, however, is where trouble for us Christian believers arises. For on the one hand we have had an essential union with God effected in our spirts, but on the other hand we simultaneously continue to carry with us that which we had obtained from our physical birth, which is to say, our natural energy. So the question now arises: what are we going to do with this latter power?

With perhaps a few exceptions the tendency with each of us has been this: heretofore I employed my mind in pouring over history, business, or chemistry, over questions of the world, over literature and poetry, etc.; I quite naturally studied with my keen mind, using it to obtain information or else to gain some inspiration from such studies. Now, however, my desire or goal has been drastically altered, it henceforth being the things of God. Nevertheless, I employ the same mind in relation to God and His interests. I have changed my subject of interest, but I have not changed the mind of my heart. Although the subject of interest has been utterly changed (I praise God for that!), that development is not sufficient—from God's perspective. For we are utilizing the same power or energy to study Corinthians and Ephesians which we previously employed in our pursuit of history, chemistry, and geography. Our utilization of that power is not the will of God for our life in Christ. God will not allow that. The trouble with so many saints is that they have only changed their subject of interest, they have not changed the source of power and energy with which to pursue that new interest. My singling out here of the mental power from among the various expressions or abilities of the soul has only been done by way of illustration.

We shall find that there are many other soulical powers we carry over into our attempts at taking up divine service. Take the ability of eloquence. There are some people who are born orators: they can present their reasonings, thoughts and arguments very well. Then they are converted and automatically assume they can employ the same power for preaching. It is now a different subject of interest but the same power is being used.

We cannot see or discern this simply by hearing. God must come in and put His finger on whatever He sees which is unacceptable and say to us: Look here, this power source is natural; it is what belongs to the old creation; it must go. Unless God points out to us the particular energy source as natural which we are utilizing in our attempt to serve Him, we cannot see, recognize, or realize it. God must come into our lives and do whatever is necessary in the most deliberate and thorough manner; such that it shall rule out the use of whatever is natural which we may be employing in our attempted service for Him. We must arrive at that point in our Christian life wherein we must declare: Lord, this which I have been doing in trying to work for You is unclean and impure—it lacks purity.

That word purity is a most blessed word; indeed, I always associate it with the Holy Spirit. Purity signifies that which is altogether out of the Spirit of God, whereas the word impurity conveys the notion of mixture.

Hence, the core issue comes down to this: How am I going to deal with this natural life? What is absolutely fundamental is, that I must have a revelation from God by His Spirit that will enable me to see it. For I can tell you this, that a person could understand the matter for years without actually *seeing* it. Yes, you may rejoice in the truth of what has been pointed out here but it will never cause you to loathe yourself for having used your natural energy to achieve spiritual ends; you may have also rejoiced in such teaching but that alone can never cause you to humble yourself and acknowledge your error. On the other hand, when God gives a revelation causing you to see that the natural life is that which He cannot use in His service because of its impure and corrupt character, then you will not enjoy the truth and will loathe yourself for having used your natural power to accomplish spiritual service. Now once that occurs, there will be deliverance for you, your natural energy having been dealt with at last.

I have often put forward a question whose answer is very difficult to grasp hold of. What is the reason why God has wanted to do everything? For He has done everything, indeed, as regards our salvation, and He will likewise do everything as regards our service for Him, since He will not let us have any part in it. Hence, the explanation is that if God is going to have all the glory, God has to do all the work; accordingly, if He shares with you His work, He must obviously share with you His glory. So God has to rule man and everything that is of man out, in order that He may have all the glory.

Yet there is a further aspect to all this which needs to be considered here. Whatever is out from us will never be truly fruitful nor have any real spiritual value. True, we may be used and be blessed to a certain degree, but that will not answer God's ultimate end, for with regard to His eternal purpose, which is the full end of God, unless He is the one effecting it or bringing it about, no one can do it, and therefore we are out of it altogether. Natural energy fails God here.

So once again we are brought back in our discussion together to this subject of Aaron's rod, that which had been brought into the tabernacle—the sanctuary of God—for one long dark night, and then by the following morning it had budded, blossomed, and yielded up ripe almonds (Numbers 17:8).

Here we have before us, in symbolic fashion, death and resurrection. The aspect of the death of Jesus, spoken of in the Scriptures as our conformity to His death (Philippians 3:10c), is just like the death which the Lord died in the sense of John 12:24, which speaks of what happens to a grain of wheat that falls to the ground and dies. He passed away, and His life results in many lives. God's Son died, and came forth to be many sons. One grain died, and then there are many grains. Many grains were actually in that one grain, but that grain is now becoming, not many grains but, the first grain. Once upon a time it was a grain of wheat; and now that grain becomes the first grain. So here we have the only begotten Son of God who becomes the first begotten, and we are coming forth as His brethren and have a share in His life. It is in this aspect of death that we died. We, like Jesus, lose our life in order that we may be life-imparting ones so that we may give our life to others.

Now the issue of death and our natural energy is simply this: that natural energy of ours will continue with us until our physical death, but there must be a fundamental breaking or wounding of that power and energy just as God had to touch the sinew of Jacob's thigh: he continued to walk, but he ever afterwards was lame. Yes, Jacob still had his feet intact, but his life had been touched in such a manner that from that wounded moment onward Jacob never recovered his natural energy (Genesis 32:24-32).

God has to deal with us—I do not know how, but God will—so that our natural power is cut off. With some of us He has to deal very harshly, in difficult ways, to bring us to that point in our Christian walk wherein we dare not trust ourselves, that in fact we are almost afraid to do so. We may even reach the point that we shall not want to do any work for God. In this very regard, I must relate this personal story, that after I was converted, for an entire year I had the lust to preach; as a matter of fact, it was impossible for me to stay silent. It seemed as though there was an unstoppable going forth in which I simply had to keep preaching. But then, one day that lustful energy of mine was touched in such a way that henceforth I no longer did it for the joy of doing it but because the Lord now wanted me to do it.

Let me say out of my own experience that when one's natural life has not been dealt with, a person may, for example, have a lust to preach, and yet there may be times when the Lord cannot move him to lift a finger to undertake one single activity for Him. If such be true of you, it is an indication that you are living by the natural life, because the natural life can vary a great deal. When emotionally you are set on this course, you will pursue it at full speed; but when emotionally you are set on going in the other direction, you will not move at all even when duty to God calls forth obedience. In other words, you are not pliable in His hands. In that case, God has to deal with your natural energy so that you will serve Him in this way or that because *He* wants it and not because you *like* it; that is to say, you may like the particular labor God has called you to at the moment or you may dislike it, but you will do it in obedience just the same.

It is not that I can or will derive joy or pleasure from this work such as preaching or from that work such as visiting the sick, therefore I do it; rather, it is because such labor is the will of God and I therefore do it with joy or without joy. In this way you will be coming to that place where God can have His way with you because the natural side of your energy has been dealt with. God is unquestionably out for this.

It may be a most painful process for some of us, or it may be just one wounding stroke. But God has His ways, and we must be willing to go through such experience. Every true servant of God must know that breaking touch or that wounding from which he will never recover. There must be that effectual touch upon you so that henceforth you will be afraid of yourself, you will be afraid to undertake any service for God. Indeed, you will now know what kind of sovereign dealing you will receive from God if you do move out of yourself and do it; moreover, you will know what a bad time you will have before God should you proceed to move out on your own in attempting any labor for Him. You will immediately experience God's dealing hand upon you, for He will never let you go free. And once you experience death to your self-life and its natural energy you shall come to a position which we speak of as resurrection ground. The principle of death has to be wrought out in us by means of a crisis whereby our natural lives with its power and energy are dealt with, after which God releases you onto resurrection ground.

What exactly does that mean? It simply means that what you had lost in the death crisis is returning to you, yet not as before; it is the resurrection-life principle now operating in you, strengthening and empowering and animating you by means of the life in the Spirit. From henceforth what was lost under the principle of death will be returning to us under the principle of resurrection power. For instance, if we want to be spiritual there is no need for us to amputate our hands or feet, we can have the full use of our body. So, too, we can have the full use of our soulical faculties (mind, emotion, will), but the soul itself is not our life-spring; we are not living in it or by it; instead, we make use of it. Whenever the body becomes the life of man, we live like beasts; when the soul becomes the life of man, we live as rebels from God and live apart from the life of God; but when we who know the Lord are able to live our life in the Spirit and by the Spirit we make use of our soul faculties just as we make use of our physical faculties.

But the difficulty with many believers centers around that night like what Aaron's dead rod experienced before God in the tabernacle of old. I would here mention that the Lord graciously laid me aside once in my life, it lasting quite a lengthy number of months and plunging me into utter darkness. It was almost as if God had forsaken me because nothing was happening and as though it was the end of everything for me. But, then, He brought back many things bit by bit. Now the temptation for many of us is to take those lost things back ourselves, but what is required is that there must be a full night of deathly darkness in the sanctuary. It cannot be hurried, for God knows how long the night must last. If we could have *our* way, we would want to have the experience of death and that of resurrection occur within one hour of each other, since we cannot accept the thought that God would lay us aside for such a long while which might be necessary to accomplish God's aim. We dislike remaining that long in a night of total darkness, for it might be too painful.

I do not know how long a person's dark night must be, but in principle I think it is quite safe to say this, that there will be a period within which God will feel it necessary to put you there; moreover, it will seem as though nothing is happening, that you are losing everything of self, that you are coming up against a blank wall through which you cannot pass, that it appears that every other person has been blessed and used by God but that you yourself have been left helpless and abandoned. You must lie quietly; and, yes, it is all in darkness, but it is only a night, really; you must indeed endure the night, but it is only for the night. And after that death-like experience, you will have the joy of rising up in glorious resurrection. This, then, is what I believe God is at this time desirous of revealing to us concerning the necessity of our being delivered from our natural energy.

Need to Distinguish Spirit from Soul

I believe many of us have realized that there is a terrible need of true spiritual discernment among the children of God. I would like to ask: What is the root cause of this lack of discernment? It appears that we do not have the ability to differentiate and say, This is of God! or This is not of God!—Man is doing it all! or This is God who is doing it! Why are there so many mistakes being made, in that so much which is of man is being put down as being of God? What is the reason for all this? It is simply because there is a lack of discernment regarding the distinction between spirit and soul in our lives. It is only when our natural powers have been dealt with by God that we can know what the difference between these two means, and how costly it is to enter into the reality of that difference; but once a person acquires this ability to differentiate because he himself has been dealt with by God, then every movement or prompting of the natural man in others will be noticed without any effort. If you are such a person, then you have passed through.

I do not mean to be understood as saying here that we are given to learn this lesson in order to acquire the ability to notice the weaknesses of others, but for those who labor in divine service there is the necessity for them to be able to differentiate between the natural and the spiritual—between that which is of the soul- or self-life and that of the spirit. It is not our wish to have a death-and-resurrection experience so that we can sit on the platform and criticize others in a more competent way; but we do wish to know the difference between that which is utterly of God and that which is of man who attempts to deal with the problem of his natural life at its fundamental core but can only deal with it naturally and not spiritually.

Only those who have been dealt with by God as to their natural life can discern what is of man and what is of God. I have always thought that that is the only path to having true spiritual discernment; that is to say, allowing God to deal with the natural life in ourselves. The lack of discernment in us betrays the lack of having had a deep dealing of God upon us. If we cannot see and discern in our own lives the difference between what is of God and what is of the natural man, then we can never see and discern it in others. The Lord has made it clear: the beam or plank has to be removed from *our* vision if we are going to be able to see the moat or speck in someone else's vision (see Luke 6:41-42). May God grant us grace, making us willing and ready to see and realize that there is an extensive realm in our lives which needs a drastic dealing by Him. Do not take it for granted because you know something of Romans 6 that you have truly seen the necessity for Jesus' death to have its impact upon your natural man. For as regards the earlier issue discussed of sin and sins and even the issue of consecration/surrender, too many of us are exerting that natural power of ours every day and attempting to apply it to divine service.

Some of us who have a "bigger soul" than others may have a more difficult time in experiencing the breaking or wounding of their outward man. Some of us may be well aware of that verse in I Thessalonians which is a very important and appropriate one. A word of exhortation therein declares this: "Encourage the fainthearted"; and some versions translate it as, "Encourage the feebleminded" (5:14b). In fact, that word feebleminded or fainthearted in the New Testament Greek original actually means "the small-souled"—in other words, we are exhorted to encourage the small-souled. So I believe it is scriptural to infer from this that there are those who are small-souled and there are those who are naturally large-souled, and that the latter people may have a more difficult time. We cannot blame or criticize them, but it must be acknowledged that the aforesaid observation regarding the "bigger-souled" saints is true. Let me say, by way of conclusion on this point, that God may have to deal with you in a most drastic way in order that that natural man of yours may be rendered inoperative in you.

I recall a Christian brother, in introducing me to someone, saying the following: "I understand that the Lord has used our brother here to save quite a number of souls." I quickly turned to the one who had introduced me and said, "Brother, that is the worst introduction I have ever gotten." "What do you mean?" he asked. I replied: "Do you mean to say the Lord used me to save souls? I believe you meant to say that the Lord used me to *win* souls." Winning souls and saving souls are two very different enterprises. We humans win souls as men who are being won to Christ; that is to say, in this context the word souls is another way of saying: human beings. But further, we humans do not and must not save souls, for, actually, according to Scripture, the souls of humans must be lost!

Throughout the New Testament, is there any passage telling us that we must save our souls? Does not the New Testament tell us that we must *lose* our souls—that is, our soul- or self-life (see, e.g., John 12:25, Luke 9:24)? Blessed be His name! We each must be willing to lose our soul- or self-life—to part with it, to let it go. May God give us grace to face this matter of the soul's influence, power and energy, and arrive at that point in our walk with the Lord Jesus when we can declare, I have lost it!* Nevertheless, such declaration, such an experience, has lifelong implications; for the losing of our soul- or self-life

* Of course, the author here is not declaring the annihilation of the soul or the non-use of its faculties,but the disabling of the natural life or energy that animates the soul so that it may be animated instead by the resurrection life of Christ. This is made clear by the author a few pages earlier, especially on pages 54-55.—Translator/Editor

is a continuing process of letting go of our will and obeying God's will.

Perhaps today God will place His hand upon someone and say: There is yet one more department in your life which has never been dealt with before. Even so, let none of us be discouraged; for the essential truth above all else for all of us is this: Have we experienced that fundamental touch of God upon us? Has that absolutely indispensable life-wound been received? If so, then subsequent divine touches or woundings—as God sees fit—can be much less difficult to receive or bear.

May God grant us all the needed grace.

CHAPTER THREE
THE URGENT NEED OF SPIRITUAL KNOWLEDGE

"[I] cease not to give thanks for you, making mention of you in my prayers; that the God of our Lord Jesus Christ, the Father of glory, may give unto you a spirit of wisdom and revelation in the knowledge of him; having the eyes of your heart enlightened, that ye may know what is the hope of his calling, what [are] the riches of the glory of his inheritance in the saints ..." (Ephesians 1:16-18).

"... [I pray] that he would grant you, according to the riches of his glory, that ye may be strengthened with power through his Spirit in the inward man" (Ephesians 3:16).

"For who among men knoweth the things of a man, save the spirit of the man, which is in him? even so the things of God none knoweth, save the Spirit of God. ... Now the natural [or, unspiritual; Greek: psychical] man receiveth not the things of the Spirit of God: for they are foolishness unto him; and he cannot know them, because they are spiritually judged [or, discerned, examined]" (1 Cor. 2:11, 14).

We have been considering together the important subject of how we can be used of God to accomplish not our works but His works, not our ends but His ends. We have a natural life with its natural energy or power, and it must be dealt with before God can use us. Any work undertaken for God which has its mainspring for its accomplishment the power of our natural life will fall greatly short of possessing spiritual value. True spiritual value can only be realized by God being both the originator of the work and the power behind the accomplishment of the same. Moreover, even if the work in question has indeed had its origin in God, its spiritual value will remain nil unless the power for carrying out the said work is of God as well.

Questions over this matter have probably arisen in the minds of many of God's people. For instance, some will no doubt inquire: How about Mr. so-and-so over here, and how about Mr. so-and-so over there? They have obviously been using their natural power, and relying quite extensively on it in the process; and yet I cannot see or say that they are not being used by God; have they not garnered many conversions, are not many souls being brought to the Lord, and have they not had great blessing? And for that matter, how about myself? I, too, have been utilizing my energy and power, and God has in fact blessed my work; you cannot therefore say that I have not gotten blessing. Hence, I would ask you this: Is there an absolute necessity for there to be the dealing of God with the soulical or natural man? Is it perhaps merely a teaching of man, or is it a definite truth of God?

I would remind ourselves that there are various kinds of servants of God who work on many different levels. With respect to a particular person's presumed work for God, we can never put forth the rationale of God's use or not of that work as the criterion for judging whether one is adhering to the divine principle God has set forth in His word. Furthermore, the *result* of a work can never be the standard for judging whether or not the conditions of servanthood the Lord has laid down must be adhered to by anyone today who desires to be God's servant. If He has stated that one's natural life or natural energy must be set aside, then He means it must be so. There may be those individuals who have been used and can demonstrate results—even great results, but that does not invalidate or overthrow what God has revealed in His word.

Let us turn back to the Old Testament narratives concerning Samson and Balaam (Judges 13-16, Numbers 22-24). Was Samson used by God? Who can deny that He used him? God was decidedly using Samson, but the rejoinder for us all to consider is this: Are we at all desirous of being used by God in the manner He had used Samson? Indeed, do we want to come onto *that* ground and be used? I would certainly hope not! But, then, let us consider Balaam. Did God use him? Yes, most certainly, and he even gave forth a great divine prophecy which was fulfilled. The point to be weighed most seriously by us all, however, is this: Am I trying to serve God in such minimal fashion that I shall be satisfied with the Lord using me without in the least considering my inward condition? Let us realize that it is not a question of whether God has used this or that man or not; rather, the issue is, On what basis has He been using him? When the entire generation is falling morally and spiritually and God cannot obtain any better man, He has to lay hold of a Balaam; similarly, when the whole of Israel is failing, God finds it impossible to secure a better man and so He is reduced to taking up a Samson. In either case, though, it does not signify that a Balaam or a Samson is really usable. To the contrary, it simply means that God had *condescended* to use these men despite their moral flaws.

Here is the challenge I would put to you. We of a truth can say that this or that unbefitting, unsuitable man has been used of God; nevertheless, he knows nothing about the work of the cross and knows nothing about work in the spirit. If you are satisfied with being used of God merely as a temporary instrument, I do not want to encourage you and say, Go ahead. God must open our eyes so that we shall be unwilling to be a mere temporary instrument in His hands.

"All Asia Minor has forsaken me," wrote Paul near the end of his life; in fact, none is left with me but Luke, he added (see II Timothy 1:15, 4:11a). We would perhaps declare, What a failure!—Paul has not been used at all, he has no fruits! Fancy, that the whole of what is Turkey today had left him! Yet Paul has accomplished the greatest work of all the Lord's apostles. The proof of his spiritual value to God is not how many souls were standing with him; it was rather demonstrated by the fact that this servant of God had become the very embodiment of his teaching. By the testimony of his life Paul serves as an ongoing challenge to whatever is not of God. And that is what God is truly after. He is not after that which is merely temporal and is appealing to the sight of men. Rather, He is after someone who is so utterly one with Him and one in purpose and in nature that He has got an appropriate, befitting instrument.

The Basis of Service Is Oneness with God

That, in fact, is the very point I wish to "drive home" in all our consideration together. And that point is this: On what basis am I desirous of serving God? Not as a mere laborer or someone who is employed; nor am I desirous of being someone who has been conscripted or pressed into service; but my service to God is based on that oneness I have with Him in Christ in both character and purpose. Oh, the mighty difference between these two bases! And if my basis is the latter, then I am an instrument in the hand of God for His purposes.

Returning to Balaam for a moment, we will recall that when God could not get anyone to talk to Balaam He laid hold of an ass; but that action of His does not justify us being satisfied simply to be asses as temporary instruments in God's hands for His use! For the basis of one's service is terribly wrong, yet so many are content to be used in this way. Let me reiterate that the issue here is not one of use. In my personal life I have realized that many a time when I cannot find at hand that which is suitable to my purpose for the moment, I must take up something which is not suitable. And in the cases of both Balaam and Samson God had to do just that. Many a time

He could not find any suitable instrument with whom to accomplish His purpose, and hence He had to use whomever or whatever He could secure; nevertheless, one should never infer from such a situation that that instrument was up to God's standard. Let us therefore not only be God's servants but also be learners of Him in such a way in our service to Him that He can, and will, commit himself to the work which we are doing.

The Need of Spiritual Knowledge

Now I want to say a further word concerning the soul and the spirit, for I sense very much before the Lord that the trouble with us all, and with the general Christian public today, is the fact that there is a lack of spiritual knowledge. Things are now at a very low level. Everywhere one looks, there is breakdown. Even where there is blessing one finds that it is very limited. For in actual fact, the reports of such blessing are inflated, they exceeding by far what is the true state of the matter. Moreover, one finds that everywhere men are attempting to place their hands upon the work of God. Consequently, there is so very little about so-called divine work which could really be said to be of God, and the workers themselves sense it and know it. This is not to say that they possess spiritual knowledge concerning this unfortunate situation. They alone—apart from God—are doing the work, and they know there is no real trust in God and reliance upon His power to bring about the desired spiritual results. Yes, in their carrying out the work in and of themselves by means of routine formulas they may achieve results, but such results prove in the end to have been produced merely by follow-up endeavors.

No one seems to be alive to this situation. Unfortunately, it would appear as though matters, having sunk to such a low level, have today been accepted as being quite normal now, with nobody ever seeming to realize how contrary it all is to God. May I say the following without being misunderstood? God does not mind—or does not mind as much—if we do something which is wrong, but He does mind if we do not *know* it. Let us humbly acknowledge that we, together with all of organized Christianity, are wrong, in that there are many works and much other labors which are not of God; and the underlying tragedy of it all is the immense lack of knowledge on the part of God's people. Indeed, this latter circumstance is actually worse than the flawed-works situation itself. Today, therefore, there is the definite need for the spiritual knowledge that comes from God and which can bring us to that place where we are enabled to see as He sees.

We have been talking these days about spiritual growth and maturity. One thing is certain, a man who is mature, who has been pressing on in growth, sees and knows. In consequence of this, what he says is not "I think!" or "I suggest!" or "I would think!" Not so. Instead, what he says is: "I see! I know!" This is because there is a wisdom and knowledge from God which has been communicated to him in the spirit. There is that mark of spiritual life and real communion with God upon this one who is pressing on and maturing in the Lord.

Now I would like to share somewhat as to how this knowledge is imparted to us. I do not know if you have ever had the same feeling as I have had which I am about to tell you. But many a time the Lord has called me to have touches with brethren in different places who have a desire to serve God. And the Lord has called me to minister to such brethren because of my having experienced His dealings with me personally. And therefore one such as I can generally see what God is going to have to do with this brother or that sister who is desirous of serving Him. And because of what I have passed through in being dealt with by God, it is only natural that I am able to perceive to some degree what God is going to have to do with those brethren. So many whom I have encountered have been attempting to minister to others; unfortunately, they have no idea at all what God is requiring of them if they are to be His true ministers. Have you known such brethren? And so, because they live quite contentedly, they continue on in their Christian walk without ever knowing or realizing that God has a specific requirement of them to experience His dealings before they can truly become His ministers. Oh, the lack of light! Oh, the lack of knowledge!

Many a time in a prayer meeting I have heard a young brother or a young sister pray, Lord, I am willing to do anything for Thee, and I am willing to go anywhere! These brethren prayed in a most absolute way, they indicating a willingness to give up everything to God.

Whenever I heard such prayer my heart sank deeply down; so much so that I had to restrain myself from walking over to him or her and placing my hand over their mouth and saying, Brother, Sister, do not pray that, for you do not know or realize what God is going to require of you.

Oh, how very easy it is for us to *utter* such a prayer of surrender, but do we actually know what God is going to have to do with us? It is a tremendous requirement He must place upon us. And as for those of us who have passed through His dealings with us to some extent, we will almost tremble before God in having to make reference to that requirement, knowing what we in ourselves are. Hence, there is this stark truth laid before us all: that because of a most serious lack of knowledge, there is the need for divine light to shine upon us so that we may know our true condition before God and what is therefore necessary to effect a radical change in ourselves.

How, though, is this to come about? We have to go back to the very beginning of our Christian experience. We know that our regeneration—the new birth—is effected in our spirit. When we were born again of God's Spirit, He came into our spirit; which means that a birth has been effected there. Everything outside of that birth in our spirit belongs to the old creation. All of that must go down into death. That which God has done in our spirit is what God endeavors to build up.

Being built up or experiencing growth does not have reference to the growth of the soul but to the divine life which God has put into our spirits. Growth is going to take place in that organ of our makeup—the spirit—and not in the mind, will or emotion of our soul. This is because, at this initial moment in our coming to know God and His will, those parts of the latter organ in our makeup will not be useful at all. On the contrary, the trouble today is this, that whereas God's purpose is to give new life and promote growth and increase to our spirit, what in a humanly, natural way we Christians today are doing is reading many books and attending many different Christian meetings to gain spiritual knowledge. I do not mean to say that all this is necessarily wrong, but I do mean to say this, that too many Christians are diligently trying to take in data from the minds of other men for putting the same into their own minds. Their approach to the truth is merely for the sake of increasing their mental knowledge.

Too often the believer's attitude today is: I would like to know this and that doctrine; also, how this or that passage is going to be interpreted; also, what I need to know about this and that as yet unfulfilled prophecy; and likewise, about this and that and the other item of informational interest to me. Christians attempt to master the knowledge about many things, and once they have acquired so much information, then their mind is set and they thus think they have grown.

Yet, let us consider for a moment: What part of the person has really grown? Obviously, their soul has been enriched but their spirit has been left impoverished. No growth has occurred at all in the spirit, which surely is the place where spiritual growth ought to take place. From the very beginning of his conversion to Christ a young believer does gain a certain amount of knowledge of God and His Son because of his new birth. Praise God for that! And, yes, after ten years of contributing information to the mind of his soul, he will have increased in scriptural knowledge, in doctrinal knowledge, in the knowledge of church government, in knowing the different interpretations of this and that passage of the Bible, etc., etc., but has his direct knowledge of God in his spirit been increased? Sad to say, that part of his makeup has not increased.

It is therefore necessary for all of us to inquire of the Lord what the reason is for this lack of that direct knowledge of Him in our spirit. And to be helpful to all of us gathered here, let me explain exactly what this spiritual knowledge of which I have been speaking is. It is simply this: Because of my union with the Lord in my spirit I am able to have communion with Him in the spirit, and because I have communion with Him in the spirit I have knowledge of Him in my spirit. This acquisition of knowledge in my spirit directly is independent of everything outward or outside. No information gained outwardly is necessary for having such spiritual knowledge, no exposure to human teaching is necessary for enabling one to have such knowledge. Rather than such knowledge having been gained from the outside, it is that which arises from what is occurring inside me—that is, in my spirit, and causes me to know that I have it. Such knowledge is of the Spirit of God in my spirit. It is independent of anything and everything outward; indeed, not even the best of teachers could impart or provide any body of knowledge which could be considered as direct knowledge of God that comes to a believer's spirit by the Spirit of God.

What, then, accounts today for our lack of knowledge of the kind just described? What is the trouble with many of us believers at the present time? I believe it is because the kind of knowledge of God and of the things of God which many assume to be spiritual knowledge originates from outside our spirit. And if information of this latter kind ceases, our so-called spiritual knowledge ceases. Such ought not to be; instead, there must be that communion and fellowship of the Spirit taking place inwardly in our spirit independent of everything outside.

The truth is that the saints of God today neglect having this direct knowledge. They instead go about depending upon everything outward. Their understanding is: if I wish to be a good Christian teacher among God's people, I must read many Christian books, I need to take up Greek, I have to do this, that and the other to be well informed. If I desire to serve God, I need to consult this person and that and ask them many things in order that I may have spiritual knowledge. Hence, their knowledge comes from the outside, and if this source should dry up, they have nothing. When all is said and done, their spiritual knowledge of God did not progress at all since their conversion. In essence, their supposed spiritual growth has its source from their outer, not their innermost man: their spirit.

That is not the divine way of growth nor the divine way of acquiring spiritual knowledge. The divine way of knowledge is God's light coming into our spirit, resulting in spiritual knowledge, on the basis of which we each can declare: "I have seen God and His interests in a new and living way; in fact, I can sincerely assert: I *know* it now, for it is not that I understand it but I know it!" How true it is that there are many things concerning God and His ways which we may not understand at all; but with the coming of the knowledge in our spirit, we know them. Such inner knowledge about this and that is so certain that though we may not be able to reason these things out, we nonetheless know their truth deep down inside. Now that is the most precious and right kind of knowledge and is the rightful inheritance of every saint of God (Ephesians 1:18).

Many a time some of us have had the following experience. Things which we did not know or had not been clear about have somehow, perhaps slowly or all of a sudden, become clear to us: it seems as if a light has been flashed and we have almost jumped up and declared, I have seen it! And perhaps we may have been asked to give a reason for this occurrence, and we may have replied: I cannot explain it but nonetheless I know it! Now knowledge of this kind ought to be increased in us, for it is ours to receive by God's grace (Ephesians 1:17-18, 2:7); and such is the only knowledge which can be used in our ministry for God.

Unfortunately, too many who seek to serve God go about gaining knowledge for ministry the wrong way. If they wish to know something which they desire to use in their ministry, they will try to examine, calculate and put things together and draw a conclusion from such exercises. But Scripture makes it quite clear how true knowledge comes about. Not by self-examination can anyone know the things of God. Turning within our selves to discover or learn a certain matter will always end in failure because we can only touch our soul and never touch spiritual reality.

There are probably only two passages in the New Testament which tell us we must examine ourselves. Both are in the Corinthian letters of Paul. In the first passage we find that it is in connection with the Lord's Table. There we are instructed to examine ourselves in order to discern the body rightly, that we must examine and judge ourselves if we are not to be judged with the world. Hence, the self-examination in view here is concerned with the Lord's Table, it has nothing to do *per se* with our spiritual life (I Corinthians 11:27ff. AV). And, then, the second passage, found in the last chapter of II Corinthians, instructs us to examine ourselves as to whether we are truly in the faith (v.5 AV). Neither of these has to do with our spiritual condition. How, therefore, can I know my true condition before the Lord? There is only one way: "Search me, O God, and know my heart ..." (Psalm 139:23a); not that I search myself; not so; rather, You search me, oh God! In Your light, said David, we see light (Psalm 36:9b). There is that utter necessity of *God's* light shining upon us, and then we will see. The first light in David's statement is the light of God, the second light represents or has reference to the reality, the truth. That is the true knowledge.

God's Light Shining into Our Spirits

So what is true spiritual knowledge? That knowledge is the light of God shining into our spirits. When God's light is shining into our spirits we come gradually or immediately to know the truth or reality concerning whatever. No man can truly serve God by relying upon another's light nor can anyone truly live on another's revelation. If we are serving God we must know Him in ourselves. That is why I like J. N. Darby's translation of one particular phrase to be found in the lengthy passage in Hebrews 8:8-12 that is quoted there from Jeremiah 31:33ff. regarding the new covenant which God would make with His people—both Jews and Gentiles. Whereas many versions translate the phrase from the Greek as, "all shall know me," Darby's translation is quite distinctive:

"all shall know [M]e in themselves"! It is not something imparted; God's people know it.

Here I would like to share a story involving two sisters in the Lord from China. These two, though not exactly learned, had been learning of the Lord a good while. And one day they went into a village where a woman was possessed by a demon. The villagers asked these two sisters to cast out the demon. So they went to the woman, they prayed, and then in the name of the Lord they cast out the demon; but the demon refused to exit the woman, he simply staying and laughing at them, and even began talking with them as though nothing had happened. So they commanded in the name of the Lord again, and again, and again, and yet no demon was cast out of the woman. So they responded initially to this development by saying to themselves that they had better go back and inquire of someone what they should do. For, you see, they were desirous of gaining some helpful information from outside.

On second thought, however, they changed their mind, they now thinking there was something seriously wrong about the fact that the demon had refused at their command to exit the woman. So they tried again to cast out the demon, but this time these two sisters first began to preach Jesus to the woman, and as a result the demon in the woman betrayed himself; for the woman now spoke up, saying: "Oh, I have been worshiping Jesus all my life!" "What do you mean?" they asked. The woman replied, "I will show you Jesus myself!" And with that the woman led the two sisters into a back court where a shrine had been set up with an idol inside it. The woman spoke again: "Look here, this is Jesus!" We can see here that by this means the cunning demon was attempting to escape having to be cast out.

Now it was then that light dawned upon these two sisters, in that they realized this demon was being too clever in having attempted to pass himself off to this naïve woman as being Jesus. At that very moment these sisters saw most clearly in their spirits what they should now do to deliver this woman from her bondage to this clever, most cunning demon. They immediately took hold of the situation by speaking directly to the demon in her in the following fashion: "Now, look here! Do you remember that two thousand years ago there was a Man on earth named Jesus? He is the Son of God, and He came down from heaven. And while He was down here on earth He encountered many of your fellows, all of whom He had proceeded in driving them all out from those they had inhabited. Do you remember that?" And the two sisters went on to say this: "But, then, all of you conspired to kill Jesus, and you succeeded in doing so; in fact, all of you rejoiced together, thinking that that was the end of Him. Do you remember that? But look here, after three days this Man Jesus stripped away all the deathly powers which all of you had poured out upon Him; nevertheless, He rose up from the grave and was received back into heaven. And do you remember that after Jesus was received into glory, a proclamation was issued throughout the universe telling you and everyone else that whoever hears His name must confess that He is Lord, and that every knee shall bow to Him? Do you remember that proclamation? Now it is in *that* name that we command you, 'Be gone!'" And with that, the demon immediately left the woman!

I must confess that throughout my life in China many of us had gained a knowledge of, and had had dealings with, demons, but I had never witnessed anything which can be compared with what those two sisters had manifested; it was unique! For the wonder of it is that no one taught them. Personally I feel that their approach—"Do you remember?"—was absolutely marvelous; indeed, using their unusual technique, these sisters reminded the demon of the life, work, death and resurrection of Jesus on earth and of His victory over all of this demon's fellow demons and of the ensuing proclamation that at His name all must bow before Him as Lord of all, including this very demon, and then they ended by asking the demon: Do you remember? And that did it!

Where did that remarkable wisdom and knowledge come from which these sisters wielded with such great effect? I confess that I had never tried to help them by suggesting that method of approach. In fact, I must confess that I was greatly helped by them in this unusual incident, I never having thought up using a procedure like this in confronting demons, much less that such a technique would be successful! Now because of my having been bested by these sisters, and being quite curious about this entire episode, I inquired of them after their return how they had hit upon the extraordinary approach they finally utilized in exorcising from the demon-possessed woman such a cunning demon. Their response was quite simple: "When we were shown the idol-shrine and heard this woman's words—'This is Jesus!'—we finally saw the situation clearly and saw what was called for in defeating this demon posing as Jesus. We just knew it!"

That is the spiritual way. This is the kind of knowledge which we must have. Second-hand information passed on by others, and even others' revelation, will produce nothing. There is no power in it. What is the reason that today there is so much knowledge which is valueless and powerless? The answer is that too many of us are living in and by the soul and not living in and by our spirit. Consequently, we think, calculate, deduce, we argue and try to piece things together and then draw a conclusion. We thus believe that by our mental energies and by our mental processes we will arrive at the truths which God means for us to know. That is the way of the soul. Instead, we need a direct revelation from God who shines light into us—that is, into our spirit—thus causing us to have spiritual knowledge and wisdom for dealing with a given situation, problem or circumstance confronting us.

So what is a revelation from God? Such is the end or result of the light of God shining in upon our spirit. A light from God produces revelation and results in spiritual knowledge by which we can see clearly what the will of God is. The difference between these two ways—that of the soul and that of the spirit—in gaining knowledge is most important.

There is one question I would like to put to those who have been attempting to serve God. How do you know the mind of the Lord? With what faculty do you seek to learn the will of God? Let us be clear that it is only in and by the spirit that we can know God's will; it can never be by the soul. So whatever work we do which brings about good or bears fruit does not necessarily signify that the work done is the result of our having received light from God indicating His will. Such work must be the outgrowth of God's light having shone in our spirit producing knowledge of God's will for us.

The trouble with many of us today is that we are not receiving knowledge from God directly. In fact, it may be that because it seems as though God's will concerning our work for Him appears almost foolish, we therefore seek out someone else's opinion, then with our mind draw out some kind of conclusion as to what *is* God's will for the work of the moment, and finally act upon *that*. Yet if we truly know in our spirit that what appears to be foolish concerning our work is indeed the work of God's appointment, then we must refuse to live by the soul and instead live in and by the spirit. And if we do that, we can confidently risk everything and bank on God standing behind the work because He has committed himself to it.

Knowledge of the Spirit vs Knowledge of the Soul

Just here, I would like to illustrate the difference between the two kinds of knowledge about which we have been speaking—that of the spirit versus that of the soul—by relating an incident which occurred in the north of Gansu Province involving two Christian brothers. Now it so happens that these two brothers have been greatly used by the Lord in soul-winning. In fact, the editor of a magazine published by these two and who knew both of them had cleverly coined the nickname for them both as "the Moodys of Gansu" because, like the famed American evangelist Dwight L. Moody, they exhibited great power in winning souls. Now the younger of these two brothers had gotten hold of some of our literature and gradually came to see the difference (a) between soul and spirit, (b) between the knowledge of soul and the knowledge of spirit, and (c) between the power of soul and the power of spirit. He discerned the entire difference and subsequently came down to Shanghai to attend a Christian conference held among us brethren and which resulted in many of his past ways and works having to be changed. The other and older brother, however, did not change.

Now at that time a missionary happened to give the older brother a good Kodascope camera and numerous rolls of educational movie films; and from that moment forward, whenever he went to a village he would put up the Kodascope and screen and show a movie to the gathered people for half an hour but made it a condition beforehand that they must remain and stay quiet for another hour to hear him preach the gospel. It was by that means that this older brother was able to attract large crowds. For everywhere he went he would sometimes draw over a thousand people to hear him preach the gospel, and he certainly did preach the gospel, but always now used the Kodascope as the opening attraction.

Eventually, the younger brother, sensing in his spirit that something was wrong about this procedure, wrote him, saying the following: I do not feel the gospel needs any support from anything. I think we just have to preach the gospel and not use the Kodascope. To which the older brother wrote back, saying: The day before last I was in a certain place, and so many men heard the gospel and very many were converted; and I believe it was due to the attraction of the Kodascope. Furthermore, again, on the day before that, many other men were also converted, and it was all due to the Kodascope.

When the younger brother received the letter, he said to himself: Well now, my brother is a reasonable chap, and perhaps God is dealing with him on this matter at this very time; so I cannot judge him or criticize him. Over two weeks later this entire matter came before him again that there was something wrong; for he mused within himself on this wise: I cannot argue against what my brother has said; nevertheless, I know it is wrong to be using the Kodascope. So he wrote again: Brother, I know your reasons and argument but I still sense that something is wrong in using the movie. The older brother once more responded by letter, sending another set of conversion statistics resulting from his use of the films. And once again the younger brother yielded to the reasonings put forth by his brother. Yet still a third time the issue of the Kodascope returned to burden this younger brother's heart and spirit; and accordingly, he wrote once more. Now this back and forth between these two evangelistic brothers went on like this for a full dozen times! One day, however, God's light finally dawned upon the older brother himself, who now saw the whole issue clearly and immediately thereafter dropped the use of the Kodascope.

Now every time I recall those two brethren I am reminded of what a very good illustration their experience surrounding the use or not of the Kodascope movie is in terms of the two kinds of knowledge available and their difference. On the one hand, there is the Kodascope representing reason which argues that if one does not use that tool, one cannot witness many souls coming together to hear the gospel, not to mention witnessing the many conversions which will result. On the other hand, there is the knowledge which arises from that which is inside the believer—that is, in his spirit—which tells him the use of such a tool is wrong spiritually and is not God's will. You may want to put this sense of inner knowledge into words but you do not know how to explain it; yet there is the sure conviction inside you that despite the reasonings, the use of the Kodascope is wrong; and it is this innermost knowledge which is to be honored rather than the other.

So today I would say, especially to those who try to honor God in their service to Him: Do not assume this or that to be God's will simply because it is reasonable, rational, logical, or appears to be good or fruitful. We must *know* what the will of God is. We cannot reason it out at all.

I recall in Shanghai recently that a certain established Church located elsewhere published a long pamphlet attacking the teaching of soul and spirit and the difference between the two. The pamphlet claimed there was no difference, making the statement very strong. Shortly afterwards a brother came to me after reading the article and inquired: I would like to know if there *is* a difference between soul and spirit, for according to this pamphlet there is none! I replied by saying to this brother: I would suggest you lay this article aside for a little while, for I want to ask you a question: Is there a difference between soul and spirit *in you*? I am not asking what the article has to say about this matter, but asking whether there is a difference between these two in you. To which he declared with feeling: Yes, I believe so!

If we try to reason we lose out. The true knowledge of God and His will comes by His Spirit revealing the truth in our spirits, and nowhere else. Instead of following the sense in their spirits in determining for themselves the true knowledge, too many brethren follow this kind of teaching, that kind, and the other. They make an effort to receive the truth of God by means of the mind and reasoning of their souls rather than turning much further inward to their spirits. And consequently, one person will believe in this, another person will believe in that, and all of them receiving whatever is to his or her liking. That, however, is not the right pathway to the true knowledge of God relating to His will and work for us. The true knowledge of God is to be found deepest within, and not in the mind of the soul. No self-examination and no other effort is to be expended in attempting to find out God's will and way in one's self. Rather, true knowledge comes by the Spirit of God revealing God, His truth, and Christ in you; there in your spirit you will have the true divine knowledge.

Hence, the basic principle for obtaining that knowledge is what I have said previously. There must be a definite refusal of the natural mind of our outer man. The reason we cannot gain more of that inner knowledge is because our mind is too active. As a matter of fact, we have opted to use the wrong organ to secure the right thing, and we end up getting the wrong thing. Oh, if only we would open our eyes to God to behold that He has already effected what is so vital in us—even in our very spirit—through which we could know Him. Yet, if once we do see, we shall realize what a marvelous revelation God has bestowed upon us.

We must never succumb to the thought that because we have a mental power somewhat stronger than the believer sitting beside us, we therefore can or will become a better Christian because we have the ability to know divine things more quickly. On the contrary, all of us must come by the same way, learning everything from the Spirit in that right organ of ours: even our spirit. No mental keenness can help us, and no mental dullness can stop us. Whatever comes from the natural man must be set aside. What the entire issue comes down to is simply this: that when the natural life has definitely been dealt with and refused by the believer, the latter will find that there is a purity of spirit in him or her making God's revelation easy to obtain and see.

I do not mean to say that you and I are never left in doubt, and never arrive at a place wherein we do not need to find out the mind of the Lord; nevertheless, the point is that when that natural man and those natural powers of ours have been dealt with, we shall discover that the knowledge of God and His will are comparatively easy matters to obtain. Yes, for some brethren this ability is altogether a hazy, even a mysterious affair; but when the natural man and its powers come to stillness, they shall realize that the Spirit of God can make himself readily known in their spirits.

Being Usable in Fulfilling the Divine Plan

All this which we have considered together bears a very important relationship to what God is ultimately after in the universe. There is a divine plan, end and purpose to which we alluded earlier and which He has had in mind from even before the Creation. And He is going to bring us all to that end and use redeemed mankind to effect that plan. But in order for us to be truly usable in our service to God we, on the negative side, must be willing to say a definite "No" to our natural man and its power, thus experiencing the losing of our soul-life; and, on the positive side, we must learn to be sensitive to and receive knowledge of God in our spirits, and act accordingly. Sensitivity to God's promptings in our innermost being is one of the greatest blessings one could possess. By simply sensing it out we know it. And by having dealings with God we come to know His mind and will for our lives and for our service to Him. And that is the most precious possession we could have.

Many a time I have thought that the greatest tragedy today among God's people is that He has stirred in their spirits but they do not discern what that means. God is speaking to believers all the time, but they do not know what it signifies for them. There is an absolute necessity in those of us who are servants of God to be alive to God's promptings in our spirits for dealing with people, for speaking and preaching His word, for determining whether to go or not to this place or that, etc., etc. If we are open to God's movements deep within, we shall discover how marvelous this way works.

Finally, on the personal level I can only say the following relative to what has just now been said; namely, that what I have learned from God is that if I am alive to Him and sensitive to His directions within, I come to realize again and again that there is no need whatever for seeking outside information concerning His will. To the contrary, I could relate quite a number of instances in which God enabled me to sense in my spirit that I ought to do this or that or go here or there or say to this person or that; with the result that something very definite and specific was effected. Unquestionably, God can do this in each of His children, but it can only come about after one has learned to have one's natural life dealt with.

May God grant us the grace to be alive to Him continually, and enable us always to refuse to live by our self-life.

CHAPTER FOUR
ONE SPIRIT AND ONE BODY

"There is one body, and one Spirit, even as also ye were called in one hope of your calling" (Ephesians 4:4).

"And he gave some to be apostles; and some, prophets; and some, evangelists; and some, pastors and teachers; for the perfecting of the saints, unto the work of ministering, unto the building up of the body of Christ: till we all attain unto the unity of the faith, and of the knowledge of the Son of God, unto a full grown man, unto the measure of the stature of the fulness of Christ" (Ephesians 4:11-13).

"But speaking truth in love, we may grow up in all things into him, who is the head, even Christ; from whom all the body fitly framed and knit together through that which every joint supplieth, according to the working in due measure of each several part, maketh the increase of the body unto the building up of itself in love. This I say therefore, and testify in the Lord, that ye no longer walk as the Gentiles also walk, in the vanity of their mind" (Ephesians 4:15-17).

"For John indeed baptized with water; but ye shall be baptized in the Holy Spirit not many days hence. ... But ye shall receive power, when the Holy Spirit is come upon you: and ye shall be my witnesses both in Jerusalem, and in all Judaea and Samaria, and unto the uttermost part of the earth" (Acts 1:5, 8).

"Now there are diversities of gifts, but the same Spirit. And there are diversities of ministrations, and the same Lord. ... For as the body is one, and hath many members, and all the members of the body, being many, are one body; so also is Christ. For in one Spirit were we all baptized into one body, whether Jews or Greeks, whether bond or free; and were all made to drink of one Spirit" (I Corinthians 12:4-5, 12-13).

"Now there were at Antioch, in the church that was there, prophets and teachers, Barnabas, and Symeon that was called Niger, and Lucius of Cyrene, and Manaen the foster-brother of Herod the tetrarch, and Saul. And as they ministered to the Lord, and fasted, the Holy Spirit said, Separate me Barnabas and Saul for the work whereunto I have called them. Then, when they had fasted and prayed and laid their hands on them, they sent them away. So they, being sent forth by the Holy Spirit, went down to Seleucia; and from thence they sailed to Cyprus" (Acts 13:1-4).

"And after some days Paul said unto Barnabas, Let us return now and visit the brethren in every city wherein we proclaimed the word of the Lord, and see how they fare. And Barnabas was minded to take with them John also, who was called Mark. But Paul thought not good to take with them him who withdrew from them from Pamphylia, and went not with them to the work. And there arose a sharp contention, so that they parted asunder one from the other, and Barnabas took Mark with him, and sailed away unto Cyprus; but Paul chose Silas, and went forth, being commended by the brethren to the grace of the Lord. And he went through Syria and Cilicia, confirming the churches" (Acts 15:36-41).

> "And a vision appeared to Paul in the night: There was a man of Macedonia standing, beseeching him, and saying, Come over into Macedonia, and help us. And when he had seen the vision, straightway we sought to go forth into Macedonia, concluding that God had called us to preach the gospel unto them" (Acts 16:9-10).

I believe the Lord would have us consider together somewhat concerning the matter of one Spirit and one body as well as the subject of ministry and gifts. As was previously discussed, spiritual knowledge is fundamental to our ministry and service for God, in fact, fundamental to Christian life. We cannot have an opened heaven—that is to say, we cannot have divine knowledge communicated to our spirit—if we are living in our souls. We may be enjoying much so-called knowledge, truth, teaching and doctrine, but that is not the knowledge which comes from God. It is instead a kind of information we receive from others; and once that outside source of knowledge gives out, we shall be left helpless like a ship that has gone aground above water with nothing taking place. That kind of knowledge is not divine.

Now in order for the Holy Spirit to communicate His knowledge to us in our spirits we must have the cross of Christ working in a most practical and drastic way with us concerning our natural man. There is no question whether the Holy Spirit is willing or not to communicate divine knowledge to us. For He has been given by God for showing us His mind. The issue for us today is not that but one of hindrances. And beyond any doubt the greatest hindrance to spiritual knowledge is our unbroken natural man. If that has not been dealt with, no spiritual knowledge is possible.

We remember that word in I Corinthians 2 which states that the natural man cannot receive, know, accept, or search out the things of the Spirit. If God has made clear that the psychical, natural man or man of the soul cannot understand the things of the Spirit, then He means that even we believers cannot understand spiritual things by *our* natural man. Whatever comes from the natural man cannot understand the things of the Spirit. And that "cannot" is most inclusive; there is no exception. Some of God's people might try using their minds, keen as they are, to find out divine things, with quite a few of them afterwards thinking they know a lot; however, we must acknowledge what God has said: that such ones cannot receive, accept or understand the things of the Spirit.

Then one such person might inquire: What, therefore, are those things which I thought I did understand? To which I must reply: It is certain they are not the things of the Spirit. If by the natural man we have come to understand particular things, then it is certain that those things are not of the Spirit. Hence, a true knowledge of God is given us by the Spirit on the basis of the cross working upon our natural man.

Now I believe that besides considering together about the one Spirit, we need also to consider the one body. If the oneness of the body of Christ—the church—is not realized, we will not have arrived at what God is moving and working to achieve among His people. I shall therefore try to help us all to really see that which is known as the body of Christ; yet, not exactly the body with regard to Christians in general but especially with regard to those who are ministering to God.

One Spirit, One Body

There is one Spirit and there is one body. The body is one and must be one because the Spirit is one. If there is one Spirit there must be one body, for the one body is the expression of the one Spirit. Because there is that one Spirit—and no one doubts that the Spirit is one—the body is, and must be, the one full expression of that Spirit. We were baptized in the one Spirit into one body. The connection between one Spirit and one body is most remarkable. There you have the Spirit and there you have the body. The foundational reality is that the Spirit is one; therefore, the manifestation of that oneness—which is the body—must be one and is one. The question today is not whether there is unity in the Spirit or not: there is always unity in the Spirit; the question, rather, is this: Do we endeavor to keep that unity (Ephesians 4:3)?

But a second question arises, and it certainly is not whether the body is one or not—that is not open to argument. Instead, this second question is this: Are we going to cause or make schisms in the one body? In Ephesians 4 God through Paul makes it clear to us all that our ministry is on the basis of the one body. Likewise, I

Corinthians 12 demonstrates it to be the same, in that our ministry is on the basis of the one body since the subject of gifts was brought into view in both these passages: the gifts are all for the body.

I want us to go on to see what all this means practically for us. Yet, I do not wish to give an exposition on those verses which were quoted at the beginning of today's discussion. Instead, I only wish to utilize those verses as they may relate to the primary consideration which I believe God has for us at this present time.

The body—the church—is one with the Lord Jesus. He is said to be the Head of the body, and we are said to be its members, and our ministry is said to be the building up of all our fellow members—which is to say, the building up of the body of Christ. So as regards ministry we who know the Lord and are members of His body stand on the ground of the body to the body. In other words, with this body always in view, we stand on the ground of the body to minister to the body, to minister from the body as my basis unto the body as my object that is to be built up. That is ministry.

In the First Corinthians Letter we are shown that the ground of ministry is what every member of the body of Christ has peculiarly or uniquely to itself. There in its 12th chapter Paul likens the body of Christ to man's physical body whose various members possess diverse abilities for ministering to the physical needs of the human body. And hence, like the many-membered physical body, we who are living members of Christ's body—the church—have been endowed with diverse abilities, each of which is to be used in ministering to the entire body of Christ. For instance, perhaps one believer in Christ has been gifted to be hands for doing practical things in serving the saints; or perhaps this, that or the other believer may have been gifted, respectively, with spiritual eyesight for the body to see or with spiritual hearing for enabling the body to hear or with spiritually consecrated feet for the body to follow that member's lead—and all for the body to be built up and matured. Thus we who know the Lord are all members of Christ's body endowed with specific abilities unique to ourselves for ministering to the needs of the one body.

Yet, as this same 12th chapter of I Corinthians has also made clear, the member who, for example, has been gifted to be a *hand* cannot minister *sight* to the body, since such ministry can only be accomplished by the member who has been gifted to be eyes for the body. In other words, those body members who are eyes possess that which is peculiar to them and thus they are able to minister spiritual sight to the rest of the body of Christ.

This means, therefore, that we cannot minister that which we do not possess: we cannot give sight to the body if we are not eyes: we cannot provide taste to the body if we are not tongues. We must be that which is singularly ours if we are to minister that particular aspect of divine life which we have experienced.

To put this another way, then, ministry is based on our experience of the Lord and based on that knowledge of Him which is unique to ourselves. We most certainly praise God for the general ministry which almost every Christian can undertake—bearing witness for the Lord; but our most specific use to God is that knowledge of the Lord that is peculiar to ourselves. And such can be said to be true ministry which all of God's people ought to seek after continually before God and endeavor to carry out for the body's sake.

The Knowledge of the Lord That Is Distinctly Yours

Now before proceeding further, I want to be certain that I am not misunderstood in my use of the word peculiar just now. My use of that word was not meant to convey the notion of God's people having strange, bizarre, odd or eccentric spiritual experiences. Not at all. What I meant and still mean to convey is that true ministry to the body must be based on one's experience of having received from the Lord that knowledge of Him which is distinctly and uniquely one's own and not the result of some knowledge or information about the Lord gained from someone else. To explain it another way, one's experience of the Lord and the knowledge of Him received therefrom is—to repeat myself—peculiarly one's own, like the sight to one's eyes. Without this knowledge of the Lord that is singularly one's own there is actually no ministry for that member of the body to share. In short, every true ministry must be born out of a specific knowledge of the Lord that is distinctively, uncommonly the member's own for sharing with the rest of the body of Christ.

I wish next to emphasize here a further aspect to the matter under discussion and which has already been mentioned but only briefly; which is, that this personal, unique knowledge of the Lord has not been given by God for yourself, nor is it for the particular group of brethren you may be serving nor for the so-called organized church where you might be ministering nor for the few who may be situated around where you are located, but it is for the body. Each and every knowledge of the Lord which each member of the body uniquely possesses is meant by God for the upliftment of the entire body of Christ. If I am able to declare before God: Oh, my eyes now see!, then I may just as well be declaring: Oh, my entire body now sees! That is to say, the sight of my eyes is distinctively *my* sight, and thus it is not only my eyes which see but my whole body sees. Spiritual sight is therefore given to this or that member for the sake of the entire body of Christ and not for this or that individual member or for a few members. Hence, the sharing of every true knowledge of the Lord Jesus can never be limited to the benefit of a few but must be for uplifting the life of the entire body of Christ.

By entering upon a new plane of life as just now described, wherein we receive a fresh knowledge of the Lord Jesus unique to each of us individually and then share with all, we can be used by God to uplift the life of the entire body of Christ. Indeed, I believe that is the way God wishes to work through us. By way of illustration let me again employ our physical eyes. Sight was given to human eyes by God, but no one can deny that such sight was provided for the entire human body. By the same token, spiritually speaking, God bestows revelation to each of us believers individually in the form of a fresh seeing of himself and His Son, and hence we have spiritual sight. Yet that sight is uniquely ours belonging to no one else. However, like sight bestowed for the entire physical body, this gift from God of spiritual sight is meant to be passed on to the entire spiritual body—the body of Christ—for its uplift as a whole! And thus the body of Christ has received a fresh new portion of spiritual sight which in experience it had never had before. So the greatest spiritual ministry of today is that being rendered for uplifting the plane of life of the whole body of Christ.

Let us pause for a moment and become very practical here in our approach to this matter under discussion. Here is a brother in Christ. God leads him through deep waters, sufferings, testings, trials and difficulties, and through all these he emerges gloriously with a new knowledge of the Lord, a knowledge totally peculiar to himself. In fact, that is the correct use of that word peculiar—it being indicative of a knowledge that he has uniquely learned which in a sense others did not, and perhaps could not, learn. In a way which is singularly his and his alone, he has learned something of the ways and working of God. Moreover, a further practical point is this: Is this which this brother has experienced going to go no further and simply end there with that member of the body? If he is a faithful servant of God, the result of his experience is going to be imparted to the whole body of Christ. And thus, one member of the body learning something of the Lord experientially can mean, if shared, that the life of the body is uplifted.

I hope that I may make the following observation without being misunderstood: that there is a kind of divine ambition which pleases God. Let me explain what I mean by this. I believe that the plane or level of life in the body of Christ is continually receiving from the Head that which is meant for supplying this body; nevertheless, the state or condition of that level of life depends upon how the members are conducting themselves. If the members of the body take in more of Christ by experiencing Him more and imparting the same to the body, then the life of the body rises to a higher level. Accordingly, the greatest service or ministry body members can render is this: that they allow God to do that in them which is unprecedented, He never having been permitted to accomplish that in a member heretofore. Yet I do not wish to cause us to fall into self-conceit, but this is what I meant in alluding a few moments ago to what I termed a divine ambition pleasing to God. Let us be willing and ambitious to permit God to achieve in one of us what He has not yet found it possible to do in other members; and if such becomes a reality in that one, the latter can be used by the Head of the body to create a new plane of life in the body. I have not the words to express this satisfactorily, but I nonetheless see that this is what God is after in His Son's body.

We can see evidence of this having occurred by observing the experience of quite a few saints. Typically, it is when the entirety of God's people have sunk to living at a lower plane of spiritual life that such saints have been willing to be taken in hand by God as instruments of His in positively reversing the situation. Such saints have deeply sensed within themselves that something is not right in the body of Christ. Indeed, they have sensed that the level of spiritual life therein is so low that no one seems to realize just how poor a level its condition has sunk to, with the generality of God's people having become satisfied by thinking that because they have been saved through the blood of Christ and are now all Christians worshiping the Lord, all is fine and well. Not so with this and that concerned saint, who are willing to open themselves up to suffering for Christ and His body's sake. Such members of the body are prepared—if necessary—to experience suffering, testing, trial, difficulty and hardship in order that God may bring these willing members to a new and distinctive knowledge of himself and His will which is above that of other members. And, therefore, through these concerned saints the body of Christ is enriched and the level of life is enhanced. Such is true ministry: the result of my being divinely ambitious to open myself to God for Him to do a work in me which is unique to myself. And because of that particularly unique work accomplished in me, I have something to contribute to the body of Christ for its upliftment.

Let us not think that all ministry to be found in Scripture is the ministry of the Lord. Praise God, there is that; but the ministry of God's word is based on the ministry of the Spirit of life. Without that, such ministry is mere letter and is death (II Corinthians 3:6); it is mere teaching and doctrinal truth. No matter how vast a knowledge one has of God's word, it will never constitute that person being a true minister of God. Only one who can minister Christ can be called a true minister of God. Have you something of Christ to minister, something which you know is distinctively yours, that which the Lord has brought you through and which you uniquely possess?

Allow me once again to illustrate what is being said here by referencing the eyes of the human body. Sight in our physical eyes is what they uniquely possess: the eyes, and no other member of man's body, possess sight. In like manner, you who would exercise true spiritual ministry must come into possession of that which, by experience with God, becomes uniquely yours and which no other member of the body of Christ possesses for imparting to the rest of the body. And hence, what you have distinctively received in your experience of Christ is what constitutes true ministry. That is why the ministry which we are considering together at this time is that which is altogether intensely, seriously spiritual: one cannot enter into true spiritual ministry by simply joining, as it were, a circle of ministers; rather, entrance comes about through having spiritual experience with the Lord.

We are told in God's word that there are diversities of ministries but one Lord. Everything therefore springs from Him, and thus He is the spring or source of all the ministry to be imparted just as the Spirit is the spring of all the gifts to be exercised. Oh, without a knowledge of the Lord peculiar to ourselves there is no ministry whatever for us to impart to the body of Christ.

God Seeks True Ministers

It all comes down to this, that God is seeking for *true* ministers to work among His saints. The reason some of us who would be God's ministers have had to experience such difficult times before Him is because He cannot give us that which is real, true and substantial without bringing us through a crucible of hardships, difficulties and other trials. God must lead us through testings of all sorts so that we may know Him in a most practical, experimental way. Only then will there be ministry which is true and real. That is why all God's people in Scripture who have a divine ministry have a history with Him. Hence, to put it briefly, if there is no history there will be no ministry.

So you who would minister must not be surprised if you are truly placed in God's hands for Him to then lead you into experiences which you would never have expected. There will be situations, events and circumstances which will puzzle you, cause you to question whether you are truly of God or not and question whether you are wrong or right; you may even wonder what is the trouble with you, that whereas so many others are being used by God, you seemingly are not. They appear to have fruit and appear to go on so smoothly; and yet, with you it seems as though everything goes crooked, nothing in your walk with God being straight.

You will indeed be puzzled, but please bear in mind that God is training you for His ministry. He has a definite end in view, to bring you into knowledge of himself which you could not learn otherwise. And once you have arrived at God's end, you shall discover that not only have you personally benefited but most importantly the body of Christ is continually being enriched.

We must not think that this aspect of being personally tested is unimportant. I have to confess that in a very small way the Lord has sometimes led me into some difficult situations—so difficult, in fact, that I have felt that I might just as well be unfaithful and let go this time; for are there not many chances later to make up for this one lapse? But God "drives home" the matter most strongly with me. Yes, such lapse in faithfulness may not matter very much with you and me personally, but it constitutes a substantial loss to the entire body of Christ. Are you really willing for the whole body of Christ to suffer as a result? If not, then happily you have learned that the issue involved has far greater implications than anything personal for yourself. Every test you and I pass through is not to be viewed as merely a personal one but is actually to be seen with the body in view. If one of its members can come through a new though perhaps difficult spiritual experience before God with an ability to rise to a new level of life, then there will be something which all the other members of the body of Christ can enjoy.

Think of the trials and experiences of saints during the past fifty or hundred years; many have been brought into something new. Take, for example, the testimony of Georg Müller [i.e., George Mueller] from Prussia who early on came to England and settled there for the rest of his life. Oh, how he learned of God concerning faith! He pressed on as merely one member of the body, yet today how many brethren have been living by faith because of him! He received and experienced a new level of life from God, and the body has immensely profited ever since by that measure of life having been received by him personally and then imparted to the body of Christ as a whole. Such is true ministry.

Let me say again that having true ministry means that I go before God, willing to be dealt with by Him in facing various tests and trials, and by these experiences learning things of Him and having a fuller knowledge of the Son of God, and through it all I receive a fresh measure of life; and yes, it is firstly for myself, but in time that constitutes my ministry to the body. Without this history with God there can be no ministry but is altogether empty talk, it resulting in a person giving out certain truths passed on to him previously as information and passed on to yet another as information, and so on. Whereas true ministry is receiving life from Christ by means of various personal experiences before God and then imparting the same to the body.

Must Minister on the Ground of the Body

We now come to a further point to be considered. Where do we who would be God's ministers stand personally? Yes, at the beginning the object of our ministry has been to serve the body. God's work is always for the body, is always with the body in view. So, where must we stand personally? You and I, as God's ministers, must stand on the ground of being members of the body of Christ. Mark you well, not members of an organization, nor members of a religious system, but members of Christ's body. Yes, ministry is for the body, but at the same time ministry is undertaken on the ground of the body. As I have said previously, it is a matter of our being from the body to the body. In our discussions together thus far we have seen a little concerning what it means to be *unto* the body; and hopefully we will now see a little what it means to be *from* the body.

Let us realize that the Lord has no ministries outside the body. In those passages which were read earlier concerning the ministries and the gifts for ministry, God through Paul has made it clear that those who engaged in such ministries or exercised such gifts were all fellow members of the one body of Christ. Back in Paul's day they served one another on the basis or ground of being fellow members of the one body. That is why no one could truly serve God unless that person did so on the ground of the body; for if anyone ministered to the body on the basis of some other ground, such ministry was not a sharing in life.

Let me illustrate in the following manner what is meant by this term ground. My hands have ministered to me—my body—for many years. They and my fingers minister to the members of my body in accordance with my physical life. Therefore, anything being ministered to me from outside my body cannot be termed true body-life ministry, for the ground is wrong. The basis or ground for ministry or service in relation to my body can only be on the basis of member to member within my physical body. In like manner is this true with the spiritual body of Christ. True spiritual ministry can only be rendered in the body of Christ on the ground of member to member.

Now what does all this come down to? It is simply this, that you who would be God's minister will not minister by taking a personal or individual or group line but take the line of the body. The body and not a person or group of persons is the proper basis for rendering ministry.

We have been talking about the life of the Lord; about the life of the Spirit; about the crucifixion of the natural man and our refusal of its life, mind or energy; about our service to the Lord; and especially about the cross of Christ—how it operates in us as a practical working principle and not held up simply as a teaching. But the question is, What is to be the result of all this? God does not make you and me crucified men and women and put us in the body of Christ one by one. Crucifixion for the believer is simply the flesh being dealt with so that there will be no hindrance to the unity of the Spirit in the body.

What the Body of Christ Is

I recall that on one occasion I and several other brothers were traveling together by auto in inland China. And during our conversation in the car there arose the question, What exactly is the body of Christ? We wished to come up with a definition which would be clear, accurate, and simple so that brethren could easily understand what it is. And this was what we concluded in declaring, from the perspective of whoever is voicing the definition, what exactly the body of Christ is: It is the Christ in me plus the Christ in you plus the Christ in every other Christian; but also, minus: the flesh in me, the flesh in you, and the flesh in all other Christians. Here, then, in my judgment, is what the body of Christ is in its simplest description; but let us ever bear in mind that the plus is not enough; there must always be the minus element in the definition. The minus part means, of course, the doing away of all that is natural in us; thus leaving what remains: all that is of Christ in each member combined together. Hence, by that means, one arrives at what the body of Christ is in its essence. The body is that which belongs to the Spirit to the exclusion of the flesh.

Individualism Must Go

Now we each of us may have initially assumed that the Christian life is an altogether individual matter: in time I allow God to deal with *my* natural man—with *my* flesh. However, when my individual flesh has been dealt with, I discover I am part of a tremendous whole: I learn that I belong to a spiritual entity—the many-membered body of Christ—to which every other Christian belongs as well.

Our life in Christ is not an individual matter. When the "no-good" flesh (Romans 7:18a) is present, our Christian walk is indeed very individualistic in its manifestation; we each will pursue the most individualistic paths; but when my "no-good" flesh has been dealt with, I come to realize that the life of Christ in you corresponds to, and gravitates towards, the life of Christ in me and likewise gravitates towards everyone else who possesses Christ's life. And soon thereafter the individualism of the flesh departs naturally, spontaneously, without any effort on my part.

Let us ponder this point well: that God is seeking to have a body for the expression of the life of His Son. A table I have made may express my skill as a carpenter, the house a family has had built may express their talents in design; but it is only a body which can express our very selves. Likewise, only a body—the body of Christ—can express the life of the risen, ascended triumphant Son of God. A body which is truly living is what God is after. Hence, we who are members of that body and ministers of Christ, cannot pursue individualistic paths. Rather, having been dealt with by God in terms of the natural man and the flesh in ourselves, we immediately discover that each one of us is a part of a whole: we have lost our self-life in the body of Christ, we are one in Him by the one Spirit.

Now for the practical effect of the believer's discovery and acknowledgment of the foregoing truths, one's attitude, approach, and conduct within the body becomes very different from what they had been before. Immediately upon my realization of it all, I as a body member will no longer be concerned whether I myself am the one undertaking a given work of ministry or not. The attitude and approach to such concern now is whether the Head has got His body doing the work. It means that all feeling of jealousy will go, any spirit of competition will go, my private individual works will also go. All such petty matters and smallness of views will depart the scene. For it no longer matters whether I am the member in the body ministering or another member is the one who does. The preeminent attitude to take is this: we Christians all belong to, and are members of, the one body of Christ. And this thus means that a jealous attitude will not arise if this or that member has the approval of the body in taking on a substantial amount of ministry. For if it is one body it is one in Spirit. Instantly, therefore, the individualistic attitude and/or work disappears, for it is now all right for the Head to set me aside or place me in an obscure corner or on a back seat. It is indeed all right, for I will not struggle or fight in pursuit of place or position because as long as the ministry is accomplished on the ground of the body and by the body, I still have a part in it. Instead, all ministry or work of an individualistic sort will and must go. There is no such thing as individual ministry or service to be seen in the Scriptures.

The Principle of Body-Life Practically Observed in Paul's Ministry

Earlier we read together those three passages from Acts chapters 13, 15 and 16. In those passages we can readily observe the principle of the body being carried out. We first see that several prophets and teachers of the church in Antioch are gathered together, along with two other brothers: Saul (soon to be called Paul) and Barnabas. The Holy Spirit called these two brethren and sent them out to be the first missionary-apostles (i.e., sent-out ones) for going out to do His work. However, the Spirit made His calling of these two brethren quite clear as well to those others from among the body members—the prophets and the teachers—who were gathered together there. Do we see the two sides of the body principle in effect here? On the one hand, whatever individuals are involved (in this case, Barnabas and Saul) must certainly have the leading from the Spirit of God; on the other hand, He does not leave the matter up to these two individuals by themselves but makes these individual callings clear as well to those other and representative members of the body of Christ—the prophets and the teachers—who were gathered together with Barnabas and Saul.

I especially like the substance of those two verses 3 and 4 which are put together back to back: *they* (i.e., the church) sent them; and *the Holy Spirit* sent them. Here we witness a church working in accordance with and in conjunction with the Holy Spirit, and thus we behold the body principle in beautiful operation. Yet it is not the body taking the initiative but it is the Holy Spirit doing so through the body. If the body principle is to operate properly it must be exhibited as an expression of the one Spirit in the one body. The overall authority over a given matter rests with the Spirit, but the body expresses the result or essence of that authority. It cannot be one member or a few members expressing it.

The Laying on of Hands

How did they send them out? They laid their hands upon Barnabas and Saul and sent them forward. Now what is the meaning of the laying on of hands? Do I mean to interpret this action as implying that these two brethren were ordained to preach the gospel? Now we must turn back to the Old Testament to learn what the laying on of hands signifies, since this practice has its origin during that period of Jewish history. Back then the laying on of hands had more to do with animals than with men. All the Levitical animal offerings had hands laid upon them. Were these animal sacrifices ordained? Obviously no!

What, then, is the meaning of laying one's hands upon such animal sacrifices? That action was done for the purpose of identification. Here we have a bullock or a lamb which is going to be killed and offered up to God as my personal offering. I lay my hands upon it to identify myself with it so that in its being killed it means that I am being killed, in its being offered up it means I too am being offered up. In the placing of my hands upon it my action signifies that I am one with the animal sacrifice, and that its being placed on the altar signifies that I myself am being placed there.

Hence, such is the meaning of the laying on of hands. There is nothing official surrounding the practice. It is only with the rise of the Roman Church that there developed the modern religious idea of the laying on of hands. In the Scriptures there cannot be found anything of an official character about it. The practice is but an expression of my spiritual identification with the one upon whom I lay my hands.

So these brethren in the Antiochian church laid their hands on these two sent-out brothers. You two are going forth abroad, but so do we! Whatever you pass through and experience, remember that we pass through all of it with you! Indeed, the body of Christ passes through it all with you! The mission you two brethren are going forth to carry out is not an individual work, it is a work that is to be accomplished on the ground of the body. It is not that you two are going out to distant lands and perhaps to suffer, or to do something by yourselves, and we remain behind. Not so! We place our hands on you to signify that where you go, we go; that where you are, we are going to be with you!

Here, then, we see the body principle being displayed. Hence, no one can do any work for God without the reality of the laying on of hands. From this we come to understand that we cannot work along individualistic lines or conduct ourselves as freelancers. Ministry must be on the ground of the body and nothing else. Yes, whatever ministry, service or work I undertake to do must begin with the Holy Spirit's call and then I move forward—yet, not only with the Spirit but also with the body. The Holy Spirit makes the Father's will known in a given circumstance or situation, next the body of His Son falls into line with that knowledge, and then we each find our true place in the body of Christ.

The Separation of Paul and Barnabas

Let us now return to those two brethren who were sent out; later, they returned to the church at Antioch, stayed a while, and then sought to go out again as apostles. This is recorded for us in Acts 15, from which record we learn that a very warm argument erupted between them, with Barnabas insisting on taking his nephew John Mark with them as before. We do not know whether this instance stemmed from the blood-family tie or not; nevertheless, Barnabas insisted upon having Mark with them whereas Saul, now Paul, strongly demurred.

Paul's attitude towards Mark was not one of wanting to be harsh; for we will recall that much later on he wrote this instruction to Timothy: Bring Mark with you, for he is profitable to me (II Timothy 4:11b). There was nothing personal towards this younger brother in Paul's disagreement with Barnabas. As the Scripture passage makes clear, Paul believed, based on Mark's conduct on the previous apostolic journey, that it would not be wise to include Mark on this next journey in view of his having withdrawn from the work when things had become too difficult for Mark to handle in a responsible manner. This young man had been tested previously and had proved himself unfaithful. In Paul's view, therefore, it was better to leave Mark alone for a while till more maturity was exhibited.

On his part Barnabas refused to heed Paul's advice and, taking Mark, separated himself from Paul and went elsewhere. On the other hand, Paul chose Silas and went forth, having been commended to the grace of the Lord by the church brethren. Significantly, there is no mention whatever of the Antiochian church brethren's attitude and relationship towards Barnabas, he having gone on his way without their commending him and Mark to the Lord as they had done with Paul and Silas. Throughout this entire episode John mark had been merely a passive observer who took no active part in the proceedings. It was Barnabas and Barnabas alone who did.

Please bear this in mind: Barnabas had gone out this second time on his own along an individual line and not on the ground of the body, never to be mentioned again in the Scriptures. He may have done much thereafter in continuing to serve God, so to speak, in saving souls; but God's word drops his name and activity from the narration of the early church's ministry and service to God. In contrast to that, after this episode's recording in the 15th chapter of Acts, it is Paul who is seen in the Scriptures as going on in ministry. Both the Holy Spirit and God's word continue to take notice of him and not Barnabas.

Here we have the body principle in operation again in relation to ministry and service; whereas ministry which is undertaken along individualistic lines has been ruled out by the Holy Spirit. So if we attempt to do any work or service for God along an independent line, or along the line of an organization or a religious system, or along any other line than on the basis of the body, we shall find that the Spirit will not take notice of such in a positive way but will rule it out. Yet I do not mean to be thought of as saying that there will be no blessing bestowed upon such endeavors; nevertheless, I am saying that such activity does not represent the full thought of God. I would therefore ask this of ourselves: Would any of us wish to serve Him without doing so according to His full thought?

Guidance and the Body Principle

There is yet a further aspect to the body principle, which is that of guidance; and it is presented to us in a most precious way in Acts chapter 16. And the centerpiece to its presentation is the night vision Paul had been given by God of a man standing and calling out for the apostle to come over to Macedonia to render spiritual help there. So, reporting the vision to those with him, Paul and his party sought to go there. In fact, the pertinent verses in the Biblical narrative of this event clearly indicate that, yes, Paul was the one who "had seen the vision"; but then, the Scripture reads: "*we*"—that is, those with Paul—"conclud[ed] that God had called *us*" to go to those first Europeans and "preach the gospel to them." Now *that* is a reflection of the body principle in practicality. It was not the case of Paul saying to his companions: "Look here! I have seen a vision of this man begging for us to come, so let us go." Not so. It was not that he attempted to push or pressure his fellow brethren along. Instead, we notice that though God spoke to one individual brother, all the rest of the brethren had to see and agree together as to what such speaking meant.

Having said all that, however, we must acknowledge that sometimes God may only give a vision of his will to one individual which others must accept. Even so, though the knowledge of His will has been given to an individual believer, the body's movement is not based on that one member of the body of Christ. On the contrary, the movement forward is taken because of the corporate seeking of God by the body.

Ministry Is from the Body to the Body

By way of conclusion, I would like to drive home the following point: If we truly want to serve the Lord, let us seek to fulfil one very essential condition—that all our movement is on the basis of the body and our ministry is to the body: that is, from the body and to the body. Whatever we do which falls short of this requirement has fallen short of the thought of God. The cross at work in us, as well as the resurrection life and the power of the Holy Spirit being enjoyed by us: all is for the body and to the body so that there may be a ministry of the body. May we therefore not be found lacking in this respect. May God save us from all that is natural, but also, may He save us from all that is individualistic. We should now know the hatefulness and harmfulness of the natural life.

Let us see that the independent, individualistic life has to be dealt with. May God see to it that we have full protection, a full movement, and a full oneness of the body. May we be brought into the full knowledge of what it truly means to have the laying on of hands, and to undertake ministry and all other spiritual activity in relation to the body so that we may be brought into all that God wants us to be—true ministers of His.

CHAPTER FIVE
FORSAKE ALL TO SERVE GOD

See the Glory of Serving God

Nowadays there is a phenomenon among some, if not many, of God's children who consider that in serving God they are somehow bringing honor to God. What ignorance and what pride! Today I would ask you, Have you seen that shining glorious face on the throne? Unless we really see the glory of God on the throne, we are unable to forsake all. Man's eyes behold the loveliness of the world as well as the preciousness of mammon: all people are very much interested in the things of the world. Who, then, can forsake them?!? Nevertheless, should a person have seen God's glory, he would be as the apostle Paul who considered all things as refuse for the excellency of knowing and gaining Christ (Philippians 3:7-9).

You who know the Lord, do you feel it is too early in your Christian walk to forsake all and serve God wholeheartedly, or do you sense it is too late in your life to do so? What is necessary for us believers to realize is that the world can actually only give sorrow and pain and remorse, and that for a child of God to forsake the world is truly a worthwhile endeavor—no matter at what point we may be in our Christian life.

Inasmuch as we are talking about absolute consecration, some believers may feel themselves inadequate. This is because they have not seen the glory which can be theirs in serving God. Hence, they opt for returning to the world, not unlike the children of Israel who preferred to return to Egypt because they had not seen the wonderful Promised Land of God. If you have sensed the glory in serving God, and even if you were just a young man, you may have led many to Christ. When Paul was still a relatively young man, he, thinking he was serving God, persecuted the church, having obtained the authorizing document from the Jewish high priest of his day that permitted him to go to Damascus and capture Christians. But when on his way there the glory of God appeared to Paul, he fell to the ground and began to understand what true service to God is.

Perhaps you had genuinely consecrated yourself with tears, and before your tears had dried, your heart was already full of joy. This is because the deepest joy is always a tearful one; for at that moment you felt ashamed that your consecration had not been adequate and qualitatively good enough. You realized that nothing you could give would be above His worth. This revelation alone enables you to alter the demeanor and the level of discrimination in your life. You are not following other people. You are discerning that it is actually God's grace which is upon you in *His* willingness to accept your consecration. This is called knowing Him in consecration and this was the consecration of the early church.

Some of us may think that giving a little money is treating God well, we not realizing that for God to be willing to accept our consecration is a matter of His mercy. I know of two young believers who are somewhat clever and have some social standing. Consequently, they are very proud, they thinking that for them to serve God will bring Him great honor. In fact, I overheard them say: "People like us who could readily occupy some positions in society have now come to serve God instead." Upon hearing this, I told them the following: "You are wrong in assuming such an approach to service for God, for during nearly two thousand years the church has had many brethren who had served God who were better than you. This was because they knew and appreciated the preciousness and the glory of the Anointed One. They never looked upon serving God as being a small thing; rather, they thanked God for His mercy in having been willing to pour down fire, as it were, in accepting the service of poor sinners such as they considered themselves to have been. You two who are the blind, do you not know that the day will come when the One whom you consider as being well-treated and honored by your humbling yourselves to serve Him shall be the One who is going to be welcomed in glory as God's Anointed! Do ponder well who it is who is treating whom well!"

Let us fall down, kneel and even prostrate before God, entreating Him to allow us to serve Him. Should He accept our consecration, it is due to His mercy and grace towards us. For consecration is actually we receiving His grace since it is God who condescends to accept us. We need to bow our heads and say, as Mephibosheth said of himself to King David, "What is thy servant, that thou shouldst look upon such a dead dog as I am?" (II Samuel 9:8) God is so great; He is the Lord of the universe; yet lowly men may serve Him! O you who are the proud ones, you may boast elsewhere, but before God you cannot be proud and boastful.

Let me relate a story here to illustrate what has just now been said. I had a friend and brother in the Lord. During the Sino-Japanese War (1937-45) he was in Chungking [Chongqing]. One day Free China's President Chiang [Chiang Kai-shek] invited him for evening dinner. Afterwards he came and excitingly told me about the entire evening. Two months ago Mr. Moule* wrote him a letter, asking him a question. He came and told me about

* This could very well have been Rev. H. W. Moule who, with his wife, had been (Anglican) Church Missionary Society missionaries at Hangchow (now Hangzhou) near Shanghai and who returned home to England shortly after World War I (ended 1918). Rev. Moule's father, George E. Moule (1828-1912) had himself been a longtime Anglican missionary in China (1858-1911) as had been the latter's brother Arthur E. Moule (1836-1918) during much of the same period in China. However, Rev. Moule's most famous relative in this highly prominent British Church family was his uncle, Handley C. G. Moule (1841-1920), youngest brother of George and Arthur Moule. Well-respected Cambridge University professor and scholar/author/Christian poet, Handley Moule had himself been one of the speakers at the inaugural gathering of the famed evangelical Keswick Convention held in 1875.

this as well. He emphatically declared to me that the President's dinner and Mr. Moule's letter were the two most unforgettable and glorious events to have occurred in his life. But I would ask you: Here is God who far surpasses President Chiang and Mr. Moule in every respect. When you are able to serve Him, is it you who know Him or He who knows you? All who know God will fall down into the dust and offer everything to God and worship and thank Him. We who have received so great a love and mercy from God in being allowed to serve Him, how much we should be thanking and praising Him who is willing to accept our consecration. Our willingness to give our all in consecration to God is not and cannot be the source of glory for us; rather, to be able and be permitted to serve Him is that which brings us glory, even unspeakable glory!

We are therefore expecting in these days that many brothers and sisters will declare before God: "This is but our little which we offer up as a sacrifice. May Your fire come down, consume it, and accept it as You did with the animals of sacrifice in Old Testament times." This is the time when we should lay down our all for Him. If we have fear or reservation, it is unpardonable. Anyone who will deceive or have an ulterior motive will become like Ananias and Sapphira (see Acts 5:1-11), for our God is a consuming fire (Hebrews 12:29). Before God no one should try to cheat. We need to be honest, offer all, and serve Him with all our hearts.

Our consecration expresses and demonstrates our estimate of the Lord. The more we treasure Him the more we shall give Him our all. We all have things we treasure. But to consecrate is to consecrate everything. Formerly the church, in fear of being considered extreme, asked that only believers' treasures be offered up; but today the church should have no fear to demand all from those who would consecrate themselves to God. When you do not know the Lord in a fuller way, you will only give Him your treasure. But when you see His glory, you will say to Him: "I give You my present as well as my former treasure. Even all my future, I give to You. May You accept them all." Unless you give your all, you shall feel greatly frustrated.

Our consecration, as stated earlier, reveals our estimate of Christ. It indicates how much we are willing to give. In the eyes of the Jews in Jesus' day the Lord was worth only thirty pieces of silver, which actually was the worth of a slave (Matthew 26:15, Exodus 21:32). This speaks to today's people that He is a slave and His purchase price is only thirty dollars. How much are you willing to pay?

Let me tell you a story. After the war between China and Japan (1937-45) the Christian brothers and sisters became very poor. At that time a brother asked the hand of a sister and they decided to become engaged. This brother came to me, saying: "I am going to be married. Up till now I have not asked anyone for assistance. I would please ask the church to help me to arrange my marriage." What he needed for financing the marriage, he told me, was quite a large sum of money. In response I said to him: "Every side these days is quite poor. Do you think the sum of money you have suggested is too much?" He replied, "Actually, I think I shall be spending too little." As a matter of fact, I told this brother that his figure was already seven or eight times more than any other brother's marriage expense. He thought for a while, then he sincerely responded with this word: "I feel that nothing is too much for her." To this I had nothing to say and gave him what he asked for. But after two months I encouraged him to sell all and consecrate himself to God. Thank God, he did.

Many a time I have felt that even should I give my all—even my life and my blood—and place all on the altar for God, it is still not enough, just as that brother had expressed it towards his engaged future wife: that nothing was too much for her. If we really treasure our God, there will be nothing too much for Him. We will consecrate our most precious, most valuable possessions to Him. He is worthy of our absolute consecration. One's estimate of Him must surpass all.

Be an Absolute Christian

We must let our consecration be absolute. Let us forsake all and follow the Lord. In Shanghai, there was a young Christian brother. Upon hearing a message on forsaking all and following the Lord, he returned home and inquired of his father what he his son possessed. His father replied that his possessions amounted to two dictionaries and nothing more. So this brother gave away his two dictionaries. The issue is not how much you consecrate but whether or not you consecrate all.

One day when Jesus was at the Jerusalem temple He observed what everyone was putting into the temple treasury as gifts to God. He first noticed the rich putting in their gifts out of their abundance; but then a poor widow came forward and gave her last two pennies. This deeply touched the Lord's heart, He commenting that she out of her total poverty had put in far more than all the others had done (Luke 21:2-4). Jesus also praised Mary's consecration for, He said, "she hath done what she could" for Me (Mark 14:8a). For the sake of the gospel and for the house—the church—of God, let us offer our all. Let us be Christians who are thorough in our consecration.

In Shanghai there was a brother who once observed that being a Christian became harder and harder for himself to handle; for, he lamented, when you are struck by some evil person on one side of your face, it is taught that you must turn the other side to him as well (Matthew 5:38-39). This brother had said this because he was one who did not know the Lord in a fuller way but lived in himself; therefore, he could not praise God but could only clench his teeth in reaction and quite naturally feel pained in the process. But if you are absolute in your Christian walk and are struck on one cheek yet you immediately turn the other, you will feel great joy when you arrive home. If, however, you live in yourself—as did that brother in Shanghai—and you consider that striking back would be unchristian, then you have no way of avenging yourself and thus you feel frustration and not joy. Only by thoroughly laying down yourself will you be glad and praise God when both your cheeks have been struck; for you feel you have been given an opportunity to demonstrate the dignity and capacity of a Christian. Hence, let us be absolute in being Christian by forsaking all, even ourselves.

Philip Luan [a former co-worker of Watchman Nee's —*Translator*] was a most giving Christian brother. After he was saved, he closed his cigarette factory. Once a brother asked him for a loan of 100 dollars. At that time brother Luan had only 20 dollars. So he pawned his only Russian rug and gave that brother the 100 dollars. Later that day his wife came home and found the rug had disappeared. Brother Luan comforted his wife by saying: "We gave to the Lord for we are God's servants. In serving Him we must consecrate all that we have."

Paul testified to the Corinthians that though he and his co-workers were "poor, yet [they were] making many rich" (II Corinthians 6:10b). He also declared to them: "ye know the grace of our Lord Jesus Christ, that, though he was rich, yet for your sakes he became poor, that ye through his poverty might become rich" (II Corinthians 8:9). We see from this latter verse that the Lord Jesus gladly forsook himself in order to make us rich. And we can likewise touch the reality of Paul's consecration in his having also forsaken himself.

The Way of Today's Church

Consecration is not only a personal or individual matter, it is also the corporate way of the church today. During the first century all the apostles forsook everything in order to serve the Lord. From the four Gospels we learn that the apostles as individuals left all and followed the Lord. And as a result the beginning of the book of The Acts of the Apostles tells us that three thousand and then five thousand were saved. This was the commencement of the church, in which all the believers followed the example of the apostles in forsaking all to follow the Lord. The entire church forsook everything (Acts 2:44-45, 4:32-35). Later on, the church gradually began to fall away until the coming in of the so-called Sacred System in which the preachers monopolized spiritual matters and the so-called laity could in consequence relax to be people of the world. However, the standard for the preachers was not diminished; on the contrary, the church expected the preachers to continue to forsake all including the world.

All of us are aware that the Roman Catholic Church does not allow its priests to marry, for it has been understood that the more their priests live a less human life, the more they could be entrusted with spiritual affairs. Actually this is Biblically wrong; for when Paul wrote of presenting our bodies as living sacrifices (Romans 12:1), he was addressing that message to all believers and not to the apostles only.

Today people expect preachers and ministers of the gospel to be poor while ordinary believers need not be in that state. This is not Biblical truth but only a notion of the organized Church. Whenever the church is in a normal condition one can easily observe that the truth of forsaking all is not limited to the apostles and the other servants of God but is applicable to the entire body of believers.

Today we welcome the whole body of believers to join the body of workers. In other words, what your thought has been as to how God's worker should live and serve Him should now be emulated by you in your serving God as well, and in the same manner. Such should be the way of the church today, in that we should all be workers serving God. Having an earthly, so-called secular profession is for the sake of making a living. Nevertheless, though we may all be filling different offices, we all are serving God.[*]

[*] Note: Message given on 3 February 1950.

CHAPTER SIX
CONSECRATION ACCORDING TO ROMANS 12

"I beseech you therefore, brethren, by the mercies of God, to present your bodies a living sacrifice, holy, acceptable to God, which is your spiritual service. And be not fashioned according to this world: but be ye transformed by the renewing of your mind, that ye may prove what is the good and acceptable and perfect will of God. For I say, through the grace that was given me, to every man that is among you, not to think of himself more highly than he ought to think; but so to think as to think soberly, according as God hath dealt to each man a measure of faith. For even as we have many members in one body, and all the members have not the same office: so we, who are many, are one body in Christ, and severally members one of another" (Romans 12:1-5).

Introduction

In Paul's letter to the believers in Rome chapter 1 from verse 1 to verse 15 is his introduction. From verse 16 of chapter 1 to the end of chapter 11 is the first section of his letter. Then, starting from chapter 12 is the beginning of the second section. In the first section, from chapter 1 to chapter 8, Paul shows us our riches in Christ; in chapters 9 to 11 we are given to see that the riches we enjoy are similar to the riches the children of Israel enjoyed in the past.

Starting from chapter 12, however, Paul for the first time beseeches his readers as to what they should do. For from chapter 1 to chapter 8, he tells them continuously what Christ and the Holy Spirit have done for them. Not once has he told them, and now us, what all of us as Christians should do. In the first eleven chapters he continuously relates what the triune God has done for us. Since God has done so much for us, Paul is going to tell us that we should now do something ourselves. There is no reason for us to do nothing.

So starting from chapter twelve Paul begins with the word therefore, thus indicating that he speaks by way of continuation: What should we believers do? "Present your bodies," explains Paul, as "a living sacrifice, holy, acceptable to God." Other things we are unable to do; but at least we can do this one thing, and that is, present our bodies as a living sacrifice.

Christians should at least see and appreciate what Christ has done for us and what the Holy Spirit has accomplished for us. Chapters 1 to 8 especially tell us what Christ has done for us. Chapters 9 to 11 speak of the sovereignty of God: what God has done sovereignly for us. Then, with all this as background, chapter 12 immediately begins with Paul saying that all these benefits bestowed upon us are the evidences of the mercies of God. Indeed, His mercy is one with His love.

Presenting Our Bodies Is Due to God's Mercies

What Paul in essence says here is that due to God's love and mercy we want to consecrate ourselves. In other words, all who wish to serve God must first be touched by His mercies. It is most difficult, perhaps even impossible, for anyone to present his body to work for God were he not first to have known the love and mercies of God. Such would be even more difficult than making bricks without available straw for the Pharaoh of Egypt (see Exodus 5). But for the one who has seen and been touched by God's mercies, his presenting his body becomes the most natural action for him to take.

To present himself to God is the first reaction of one who has experienced the mercies of God. When a person touches and is touched by God's love and mercies, he has no way to live just for himself any longer. On the other hand, for that person who has not experienced such enlightenment and mercies, that one will consider himself, his property, his very life as the most precious possessions. But once that person has received the love and mercies of God, he will no longer treasure those possessions; instead, under God's great light, he will inquire of God, "What should I do? What do You wish to obtain from me?"

Enabling Power to Consecrate Comes from God's Enlightenment

Before Paul believed in the Lord he persecuted His disciples. He obtained letters of authorization from the Jewish high priest to take into custody those who called on the name of the Lord (Acts 9:2). How proud and majestic he looked as he approached the city of Damascus; at that moment, however, Paul was struck by a heavenly light that caused him to fall to the ground. Heretofore, without the great love and mercy of God it was impossible for him to consecrate himself. But under this great light from heaven he was smitten and fell down from off his throne of pride and self-righteousness and immediately inquired, "What shall I do, Lord?" (Acts 22:10a) Whoever of us has never experienced God's mercies, consecration is the most difficult thing in the world to do; for everyone in the world loves himself and greatly treasures his life and possessions. However, today as we stand before the great love and abundant mercies of God, consecration is not difficult anymore.

Consecration: Not Payback but Reaction to God's Gracious Work

During these nearly two thousand years since Calvary, countless people have consecrated themselves to God. Although consecration has been considered by some to be "payback gratitude," we dare not embrace such a notion, for we sense our unworthiness. How awful to even think such a thought!—because what we have consecrated are but filthy rags (Isaiah 64:6). The psalmist asked: "What shall I render unto Jehovah for all his benefits toward me?" (Psalm 116:12) Many harbor the thought of repaying God, but they dare not say it but can only confess: "O God! With Your great and un-repayable grace upon us, the least we can do is to consecrate ourselves to You." Romans 12 is thus a very special chapter in the letter since it reveals how consecration is the very beginning of any believer's Christian work. So, to repeat what was said earlier, from chapter 1 to chapter 11 of Paul's Romans letter, we are given to understand what mercies God has bestowed upon us in *His* work on our behalf. And chapter 12 is our humble response—we bow our heads and say, "We are here to consecrate ourselves to You."

Offering the Body Is a Total Offering

Paul had great wisdom in asking us to offer not our hearts but our bodies, for consecration must be practical and total. To consecrate one's heart would be an action which can be rather abstract in character. Moreover, the heart can at times be peculiar and quite puzzling: yes, it can be fairly honest; but when it is *dis*honest, it can even deceive oneself. In this connection, let us take serious note of what the book of Proverbs has declared: "He that trusteth in his own heart is a fool" (28:26a). Indeed, when a person's heart gives way to unchecked emotional changes, no one—not even the person himself—can realize it. Hence, it is more practical and dependable to offer up one's little finger than one's heart. This is because a person can hold a finger in check but may not be able to do so with his heart. Briefly stated, therefore, to offer up one's body is not empty talk. Here, then, is the wisdom of Paul. Many may declare that they have consecrated themselves, but their declaration does not convey as solid a conviction about it as what Paul calls for here: that in his beseeching us to offer up our body, the apostle of Christ is as much as saying that everything in life—our time, family, wealth, any sought-after fame, all parts of our body, etc., etc.—is being offered up. In other words, by this one act of offering our body we are in fact laying upon the altar of sacrifice everything which is ours, because everything in life is undeniably connected, quite naturally, with one's body.

The Practice of Offering Our Bodies

Our offering the body includes the following three aspects: time, wealth, and strength. First, to offer the body is to offer up my time. I cannot consume my time carelessly but must use it to serve the Lord. I cannot say I have consecrated myself and yet use my time for myself. When a person's time is offered, that person's body follows, for the body can only be used in time.

Second, you must offer your wealth. There are many poor people around you as well as many poor Christian brothers and sisters. They thus all have needs. Moreover, money is also needed for the spreading of the gospel. If in a given needy situation you say you offer your heart but your wealth does not follow suit, such conduct can only be likened to that of him who, "having this world's goods," has "shutteth up his compassion," as stated in I John 3:17a. Though compassion may have been expressed in words, what good will that do if it is being shut up? You must remove whatever has shut up your compassion and then "the love of God [shall] abide in [you]" (I John 3:17b).

The third aspect involved in the consecration of one's body is to offer up its strength. Let us serve God with our hands by doing such works in the church building as mopping the floor, cleaning tables, washing windows, and so forth. It is best that these labors not fall into the hands of the servants. Today there are many brothers and sisters who have never mopped the floors or washed the windows, etc., of the church building. You may have servants at home; you may be manager of a company; but when you come to the place of the assembling of the saints, you need to learn to do everything required to maintain cleanliness and order. This is for the purpose of perfecting you so that you may learn to engage in true service.

Sometime during the second year after my conversion I was reading in the Old Testament's Chronicles that when David was preparing materials for the construction of the temple (which in the end his son Solomon built), he commissioned thirty of his men—described there as "valiant men," "mighty men of valor," and "able men in strength for service"—to be the doorkeepers on the four sides of the temple that was yet to be built (see I Chronicles 26:1-19). I was deeply moved when I read this. Not only did David commission others to serve in God's house but he himself, who as King of Israel was constantly being served by others, was likewise a valiant man who nonetheless longed to serve and hoped to "dwell in the house of Jehovah all the days of [his] life" (Psalm 27:4b; cf. Psalm 23:6b). We, too, must ourselves come forward and serve. Today our fellow workers serve God with the mouth and we must also serve by using our hands. In the church of God there is no such thing as social status or personal custom that should preclude any of us from serving with our hands. We need to make our consecration most practical.

The Three Characteristics of Consecration

The consecration spoken of in the opening verse of Romans 12 is described as presenting bodies as living sacrifices in order to serve God. And such service—as is noted in this same verse—has three characteristics about it: first, it is a body that is set apart as holy. I had a friend who was in public service during the time of the recently concluded war between China and Japan. Once when during that war period I had invited him for dinner, he said to me, "Sorry, my body has been sold to the country; I cannot freely use it for myself." Such an attitude is what is meant by our body being separated or set apart: nobody can touch it or use it because it is reserved for God to use. Such is what is meant to be separated for God, and such is what every believer should be. Second, such service is acceptable to God, that is to say, it is well-pleasing to Him. And third, such service is reasonable, in that since God has so richly given us without reservation, He expects us to do likewise. God is not trying to close the account in terms of "reciprocal quantity"; rather, He only wishes to maintain the principle of "quality"; for when God gives, He does so without reservation. Hence, as we give back to Him in consecrated service we too should have no reservation. How very true it is that our consecration can never measure up to God's in "quantity," but it should surely be the same in "quality"—no holding back, no reservation.

The Meaning of Living Sacrifice

The first two verses of Romans 12:1-5, dealing as they do with the matter of consecration, can be divided into two distinct sections in discussing the overall meaning of consecration. And the first section consists of verse 1, in which Paul directs our attention to God's work in a Christian's personal life. Moved by the mercies and love of God, the Christian in response offers himself to God as a living sacrifice. A sacrifice offered up in Old Testament times was a killed, dead animal that was laid on the altar. After its death the sacrifice was no longer of any use. Thus, any sacrifice could only be offered up once; it could never be offered again since it was now dead. Today, however, we can die not only once as a sacrifice to God but because we are still living, we can become "living" sacrifices; meaning that, as Paul once wrote ("I die daily"—I Corinthians 15:31b), we can continuously die to ourselves and commit ourselves to God on a daily basis by offering ourselves to Him as a sacrifice to be used by Him at any time. To be a living sacrifice, therefore, is the first act of service we Christians can do towards God.

Results of Offering Oneself as a Living Sacrifice

Having Spiritual Insight

The second section of Romans 12:1-5—consisting of verse 2 only—informs us of the consequences of consecration, the first of which is receiving spiritual insight that is dependent upon a renewed mind. Having spiritual insight is most essential to one's Christian life. Many brothers and sisters who today occupy positions of service in the church lack spiritual insight. They are experienced and clear-minded in worldly affairs and are sharp in business; but in the church, though they speak vigorously as they freely open their mouths, what they say cannot be ratified or approved with any amens. This is because their mind has not been renewed and thus they lack spiritual insight. The reason they do not understand God's will is due to a flawed consecration. Many consider the problem surrounding Christian service lies in the mind, but I believe it begins with the heart. It is the heart that affects the mind. The problem with the heart arises from the lack of a thorough consecration. A lack in this regard means that the Christian's judgment is unclear. If the believer's heart is focused upon wealth, it will be controlled by wealth, and hence he cannot see clearly. But as soon as his consecration becomes absolute, his eyes will be enlightened.

If our hearts seek only God's glory and God's desire, we will have thorough insight into spiritual matters. On the other hand, if our hearts are focused on interests other than those of God, our eyes cannot be clear-sighted nor can we understand His will.

Not Being Fashioned According to This World

The second verse of Romans 12 begins with "And," thus indicating that what follows are the consequences or results of verse 1's presentation of consecration. Now a second result is that the Christian is not to be fashioned according to this world or age. The English word fashioned in the Greek original means "to be molded." God's thought is that He wants you and me to shed from ourselves the mold of this age. As soon as you consecrate yourself you, negatively, drop off the mold of this age and, positively, allow yourself to be transformed by the renewing of your mind; and thus, you receive spiritual insight. Accordingly, the order here is as follows: the consecration of the body comes first, followed by the renewing of the mind, with spiritual insight following suit. Formerly you and I were very dull spiritually but now we become enlightened, easily understanding the will of God.

Proves the Will of God

A third consequence or result of a Christian's consecration to God is having or receiving a knowledge of His will. May I say emphatically that in order to maintain spiritual insight and thus prove or discern what the will of God is, you must not allow to arise any problem with your consecration. For as soon as you do have such a problem, you immediately cease discovering or understanding what God's will is because your spiritual eyesight has now been clouded over and adversely affected. You will be unable to see things clearly and will fail to see what many brothers and sisters have seen with regard to you yourself; they are concerned for you, but you do not sense it. For it soon turns out that what you consider treasure is looked upon as trash by the church and what many in the church look upon as shameful you deem to be glorious. Many a time you are quite wrong and yet you maintain that all is quite right with yourself.

Therefore, we need to learn not to be too confident of ourselves; instead, let us humbly ask ourselves this question: "I often say or insist to myself that this or that in me is right. If, however, the Lord should show mercy to me, allowing me to be more thorough in my consecration, will I continue to say or insist that this or that thing is right, or will I now confess that it is wrong?" Our consecration greatly affects our knowledge of God's will.

In Shanghai there was a sister who came to me and argued with me about baptism. She gave many reasons why she needed not to be baptized. After she had finished, I remained silent. We sat before each other without my saying any word in response, whereas she, after waiting for some time, finally grew impatient and ended up asking, "Mr. Nee, why do you say nothing?" "Well," I smilingly replied, "you have said all the reasons, so I have nothing to say except this: Your many reasons which you gave do not bring fear to my heart concerning yourself; rather, I am only fearful that you are unclear concerning your consecration to God. Can you say to Him, 'I will give all You ask for; I will do anything You want me to do'? Suppose your later consecration should be better than today's, what then would you do?" She instantly replied, "Of course, in that case, I would be baptized." From this encounter of mine with that sister we may readily discern that the source of the spiritual sickness of a Christian is not to be found in the mind but in one's consecration.

When there is a problem with a believer's consecration, even the best mind becomes unclear. If a believer's consecration has not been thorough enough, it will affect his or her thought and decision-making; it will affect his or her action. Hence, if all Christians are thoroughly consecrated, they cannot be unclear about God's will. To discover, discern or understand His will thus depends on the degree of one's consecration. This is a very subjective matter and one which cannot be ignored.

Produces Coordination of the Body

We have been considering together the passage quoted at the very beginning of our discussion today: Romans 12:1-5. And we have seen that its first verse has to do with the Christian's consecration, which is the basis or foundation for all which then follows in this Romans passage. And among the various consequences or results flowing from our consecration to God was what we just now learned having to do with knowing God's will and which is covered by Paul in this passage's second verse. Due to one's full consecration it is possible to have spiritual insight into God's will. And in thus knowing His will the Christian experiences a still further consequence or result of consecration: namely, a willingness to be coordinated with the other members of the body of Christ. This we learn from the remaining three verses of Romans 12:1-5. A consecrated person is one who is willing and able to be coordinated with other people in the church. Verse three therefore warns the Christian "not to think of himself more highly than he ought to think." Many children of God cannot be one with other brethren nor work together with them. They embrace the notion that this is because of different viewpoints and opinions existing among God's people. Actually, however, this is not the reason for their inability to be coordinated with the other members of Christ's body, for according to God's principle, His will is one and can only be one.

Why, then, do God's people have different opinions about this or that matter when it comes to their needing to be "one body in Christ"? It is my belief that this is due to the people of God having had varying degrees of consecration towards Him. When consecration is not absolute, such condition produces different opinions which hinder the coordination of the one body of Christ. On the other hand, should the consecration of all God's people be absolute, there will not be any difference in understanding that His will is that all the many brethren, who are "severally members one of another," are—and in daily practice should remain—"one body in Christ."

Our consecration must therefore be absolute in character and our understanding of the will of God must be constantly perfected—that is to say, it must be constantly maturing. For once consecration is absolute, coordination and body life become quite natural. On the other hand, if I say this is mine and you say that is yours—or if I strive for mine and you strive for yours, there will be no way to manifest God's will of the oneness of the body of Christ. Let us realize that what people of the world treasure most is their wealth, their precious possessions, and themselves. So for the believers in Christ, God's intent is for them to lay these aside. But if I should refrain from consecrating myself to God in such manner, then I shall tenaciously hold these in my hands and esteem them as I so choose.

Why is it that many of God's people hesitate to embrace—or even come to dislike—the consecrated life? Most likely it is because they are afraid of losing their freedom, for no one who does consecrate himself or herself in this manner can any longer declare that such and such is his or hers. From this, therefore, we can clearly observe how it is that things treasured can seriously hinder the unity of the brethren. In sharp contrast, none of those thousands of believers mentioned in the book of Acts chapters 2 and 4 ever declared that anything heretofore belonging to them was any longer theirs (cf. 4:32b). Indeed, none of them ever boasted before the other brethren that he or she held to a different point of view but, on the contrary, "had all things [in] common" (2:44b, 4:32c), "were of one heart and soul" (4:32a), and that "great grace was upon them all" (4:33b). During the closing period of this present age, may all brethren in Christ live out this body life in oneness and glory.*

* Note: Message given on 10 February 1950.

Chapter Seven
Know God's Principle of Work

Lord, Thou hast won, at length I yield;
My heart by mighty grace compelled
    Surrenders all to Thee;
Against Thy terrors long I strove,
But who can stand against Thy love?
    Love conquers even me.

If Thou hadst bid Thy thunder roll,
And light'nings flash, to blast my soul,
    I still had stubborn been;
But mercy has my heart subdued,
A bleeding Savior I have viewed,
    And now I hate my sin.

Now, Lord, I would be Thine alone,
Come, take possession of Thine own,
    For Thou hast set me free;
Release from Satan's hard command,
See all my powers waiting stand,
    To be employed by Thee.

—John Newton

This is a hymn of repentance written by John Newton. Although it has often been used as a gospel song, it is nonetheless a useful hymn in Christian meetings.

John Newton was born in London, England in 1725. His father was often abroad, as he pursued a career in navigational trade. The educating responsibility fell totally upon the godly mother. Oftentimes she knelt before God in prayer with John. She taught him to read the Bible and to memorize hymns. But when he was seven his mother fell sick and died due to much heavy work. This blow caused John to go astray.

At the age of eleven he followed his sailor father to the sea. For more than ten years he spent his prodigal life in foreign lands. As both a teenager and young man he followed the dissipated life of a sailor, drinking and gambling. Many times during this dissolute period he heard the gospel. Every time he listened, he recalled the facial features and teachings of his mother. His heart was touched each time, yet he could not rescue himself. He sank more deeply into sin. Later on, off the coast of Africa he took on employment in the slave trade till he himself was sold as a slave. He was so ill-treated that he attempted to flee, and thus he suffered severe thrashings. After several years had gone by his father learned of his whereabouts and redeemed him with money.

As Newton was on his way home to England by sea at age 23 he encountered a severe storm and the small boat he was on was sinking. At that very moment the Lord answered the prayers of his kind mother who had committed him to serve God. The intensely severe storm warmed his icy heart. The very shaking of the boat awakened his dying spirit, recalling as he did his past sins as well as the story of how the gracious Lord loved him as told by his kind mother: how Christ the Son of God had shed His blood and died for him and how great was His grace! He cried loudly in the name of the Lord. He prayed to God, repented, and believed in Him, accepting the Lord Jesus as his Savior. Later on, he consecrated himself wholly to God and faithfully served Him until his death in 1807 at the age of 82.

John Newton wrote many wonderful hymns, but I selected this particular hymn because it was written at the time of his repentance. In fact, among all the hymns of this kind which he has written this is the best one written by him on repentance. People often say how terrible Hades is, and how fearful God's punishment is; but God does not threaten us with His punishment; rather, He pours out His grace and His great love to impel us to repent. Many come to repentance through simply believing, but John Newton did so through utter obedience. Just as Paul's repentance was through sheer obedience, for he, too, was stricken, so was that of Newton. So we now sing this hymn as an expression of consecration.

Having Revelation Is Prerequisite for Work

"And Jehovah said unto him, What is that in thy hand? And he said, A rod. And he said, Cast it on the ground. And he cast it on the ground, and it becomes a serpent; and Moses fled from before it. And Jehovah said unto Moses, Put forth thy hand, and take it by the tail (and he put forth his hand, and laid hold of it, and it became a rod in his hand); that they may believe that Jehovah, the God of their fathers, the God of Abraham, the God of Isaac, and the God of Jacob, hath appeared unto thee. And Jehovah said furthermore unto him, Put now thy hand into thy bosom. And he put his hand into his bosom; and when he took it out, behold, his hand was leprous, as white as snow. And he said, Put thy hand into thy bosom again. (And he put his hand into his bosom again; and when he took it out of his bosom, behold, it was turned again as his other flesh). And it shall come to pass, if they will not believe thee, neither hearken to the voice of the first sign, that they will believe the voice of the latter sign. And it shall come to pass, if they will not believe even these two signs, neither hearken unto thy voice, that thou shalt take of the water of the river, and pour it upon the dry land: and the water which thou takest out of the river shall become blood upon the dry land. ... And thou shalt take in thy hand this rod, wherewith thou shalt do the signs" (Exodus 4:2-9, 17).

The one basic prerequisite for the work of service is whether or not you see as God wants you to see. Having seen, you will naturally be separated for the work of service for God. Before revelation is received from God, what you see may only be a rod, your clean hand, or the water which supplies the world of Egypt. But after revelations have come to you from God, you see quite differently. For you now see that the rod in your hand is a serpent, your hand is leprous and unclean, and the world is full of death.

Exodus chapter 4 contrasts men's view of things with God's revelatory unveiling concerning those same things. Many ask me how they can know that they have God's revelation. It depends on whether you have seen your rod as a serpent, your hand as leprous, and water as blood. You young people have sweet dreams. I hope, however, that God will awaken you from those dreams to discern the true nature of things. God had not only made Moses to see these revelations, He also asked Moses to demonstrate them before Israel so that they too might see and understand. When Moses was asked by God to go and deliver the people of Israel from Egyptian captivity, he had considered the task to be impossible. But as soon as he was given revelation, his feeling changed.

Suppose, unbeknowns to me, there is an earthworm in my cup of tea, and suppose, further, that I do not discover it till I nearly finish drinking. Later, when I begin to drink from that same cup on another day, what will be my feeling? Perhaps I will momentarily have that same sinking feeling I originally had concerning the earthworm, and so it will be every day thereafter. This is similar to what revelation provides. Formerly Moses, holding in his hand his rod daily, had no special feeling, he having sensed nothing any differently from any other day. But ever since witnessing the transformation of the rod into a serpent and back again to the rod, Moses' feeling towards the rod would forever be radically different.

Such should be our feeling towards the flesh. We need to realize that sin is not in the world but is in us. Bad things are also not in the world, for they, too, are in us. Formerly I did not have such a realization until one day as I removed my hand from within my bosom, I discovered it was leprous. Later on, each time I ever touch my hand, I quite naturally will think of leprosy. Some people pretend to be humble, weak and obedient, but they do not always appear to be such. For before they experience God's revelation of themselves, they continually appear to be humble as long as they remember to pretend. As soon as they forget, however, they no longer put on a facade of humility. And hence, they always have to be on their guard.

All who serve God should have a proper understanding of the water of the world. To quench one's thirst is, of course, to satisfy one's need. Perhaps, though, there are people who have prayed many years that they might obtain some sort of position or blessing in the world. Hopefully they will instead receive clear revelation from God to know that all such worldly satisfactions are but blood and death. If we want to serve God, we should not remain in Egypt to drink water from the river Nile, but let us instead go forth into the wilderness that we may drink of the water of life out of the smitten rock.

Here shall we truly see what we have never discerned before. All who have revelation shall say, How strange and troubling are these things which we now behold through God's revelation! What people without revelation see are only a rod, flesh in the bosom, and water of the river Nile. But immediately upon receiving the revelation given you by God, you are able to discern the true image and nature of those things you heretofore had depended on. For you now see your "self" as the greatest sin and realize the horror of the world you had loved. Let us pray for clear revelation concerning the reality of self, the flesh, and the world, so that we may do God's work of service and be acceptable and well-pleasing to Him.[*]

[*] Note: Message given on 2 February 1950.

Chapter Eight
Spiritual Sense

For God to have His way in the church God's children need to recognize the authority of the Holy Spirit. For a believer to know that authority he must rely on his spiritual sense. If he lacks spiritual sense, he cannot touch the Spirit's authority. Even if he is most honest in both words and acts, such conduct does not constitute true spirituality. Such actions may appear to be spiritual, but such is not genuine spirituality. For example, you may see men as trees or assume an organ to be a piano. In actual fact, however, no tree in the world can walk nor can an organ sound like a piano.

Unless we have spiritual sense we are unable to be obedient and thus fail in our walk before God. Many trust in their physical eyes, though their eyesight may actually be faulty. Often they fail to see or see clearly, and yet they still claim they see quite clearly, for they are very subjective; hence, it is difficult to convince them otherwise. The same is true in the spiritual realm. On the one hand, I believe that the spiritual sense of many brothers and sisters is inadequate and I therefore hope that such brethren will be open to be taught to touch spiritual sense in their innermost being—their spirits. On the other hand, as is the case with blind people to whom it is difficult to explain, for instance, the color red, so is it difficult to teach or explain to many Christian brethren how the movement of the Holy Spirit is made real to the believer through spiritual sense. Thus, it is my prayer that all of us will have an adequate spiritual sense in our Christian walk, for the exercise of spiritual sense in our spirits serves as a law governing our spiritual path enabling us to be obedient to the will of God. Furthermore, without an adequate spiritual sense the things of the spiritual life can become letter and no longer be of the spirit.

Distinguishing between Spirit and Letter

What is spirit? And what is letter? What is the difference between spiritual sense and mental knowledge? Paul's use of the term letter is not necessarily bad, for when he wrote of letter, he was referring to the Old Testament Scriptures and its law (Romans 2:12-29, esp. v.29; 7:1-12, esp. v.6; II Corinthians 3:6-18, esp. v.6). The Old Testament is indeed God's word, and only becomes "oldness of the letter" as opposed to the "newness of the spirit" (Romans 7:6b) if we Christians do not touch or handle the Scriptures in or according to the spirit that lies behind the written letter of the sacred Scriptures. Hence we see from this that even such a good thing as the Scriptures, all of which at one time were inspired or breathed upon by God's Spirit (cf. II Timothy 3:16a), can become letter that kills or brings in death (II Corinthians 3:6). Thus, the meaning of that which becomes dead letter—in this case, the Scriptures—was once communicated by the Holy Spirit, but these same sacred writings are now being read and are trying to be understood without the movement, enlightenment, or guidance of the Holy Spirit.

A person may read the book of Romans every day of the year, he may even understand all the doctrines quite well objectively, yet he may not be moved in the least by the anointing of the Holy Spirit freshly upon the words he has been diligently reading. Thus to him, the book of Romans is nothing but letter and not spirit. We may rise up early to read God's word and we may pray at definite times, but if these are only routine activities and nothing more, then these so-called spiritual exercises shall fall into being mere letter. Although there is a spiritual shell within which such activities occur, there is no touch of the Holy Spirit upon them. We need to have spiritual sense in ourselves first, before such exercises can legitimately be termed spirit and no longer letter.

Suppose on a Sunday afternoon a brother were to read aloud to his audience of Christians Romans 2:18-19. And suppose further that there is spirit in him as he reads but in me there is no spiritual sense since I am listening only with my mind. The result is that what I have received and accepted from that Romans passage is only letter. In order for me, as I am listening to that brother read the words of Romans 2:18-19, to touch the spirit that lies behind those words, I must not only have the letter of the word but also have the spirit in me, just as did that brother who had both. Only the reawakened spiritual organ in man can know and substantiate matters of the spirit; so that when a brother reads words of Scripture objectively, these can become God's word afresh to those who hear if such hearers are aided by spirit.

So subjectively, I must not only know the word spoken by that brother but also touch the spirit behind the word. If I cannot touch the spirit behind the word, his word is but letter to me. Hence, it is not a matter of whether I understand but whether I touch the spirit with my spirit.

Even if a believer can expound God's word with great clarity and all people can understand, that word is but dead letter to me if I do not exercise my spirit to touch his spirit. Suppose a doctor has been treating a patient physically according only to the letter; that sick patient will soon become a corpse. Similarly will it be the case with us in our spiritual life if we only adhere to the letter and not the spirit as well.

When someone is preaching, the first thing I do is not pay attention to whether he explains well or if his illustrations are appropriate. Rather, as I listen I first use my spirit to touch his spirit. Whether the spirit is being released is my chief concern. For a sermon to give supply to people, such depends on whether the spirit of the speaker is released to touch others' spirits; it does not depend on whether he preaches well or explains clearly. A person may speak boldly, his outline may be clear, and his thoughts may be quite good, but his preaching will be mere letters and therefore useless if there is no released spirit.

At the end of Hebrews 5 the author writes that in order to understand "the rudiments of the first principles of the oracle of God" the Christian needs to have his or her "senses exercised to discern good and evil" (vv.12-14). For a person to run fast physically he must not only be able to walk but must also frequently exercise the talent of running which he possesses. Similarly, in order to have spiritual sense the believer must not only use his spirit but must also exercise his spiritual sense. In this way the Christian will be well-trained.

To serve in the church one must do more than accomplish works for God well but the person must accompany the doing of those works with spirit; otherwise, such doing can only be characterized as letter. What has greatly concerned me about the church in these most recent years is not the presence of sin (though I am not at all careless about that) but the increasing presence of letter. Many church works done in letter and those done in spirit may look similar outwardly but the former, unlike the latter, lack spiritual reality.

A brother in Shanghai once said, "The preaching of a certain speaker whom I heard sounded all right, but I could not touch the spirit." The same can be said in regard to much of our spiritual service: it may look all right, but the presence of spirit is lacking. Our spiritual service requires more than being correct outwardly, such must also possess spiritual reality about it if life is to be ministered to others. A church may appear most zealous, may have good teaching, and may be quite orderly; but if no spirit is there, all such aspects of church life are but letters. A church must not only appear spiritual outwardly, it must also be in spiritual reality.

In a verse which I have already cited from II Corinthians, Paul declared this: “the letter killeth, but the spirit giveth life” (3:6c). The apostle was opposed to letter, and so must we be. We must recognize that whatever in ministry or service to God is without spirit is only letter. We cannot say because we preach spiritual doctrine, therefore, we are spiritual. Not necessarily so. To be spiritual we must have spiritual reality. And for the church of Christ to be in spiritual reality, all of us, who are members of His body, must learn to have, and then exercise, spiritual sense.

In the church meetings, in listening to messages, in praying, or in proclaiming the gospel, we must learn to keep our spirits alert. If another believer has spirit but our spirit does not respond, something must be wrong with us. If we cannot use or exercise our spirit, our spiritual life must be in a death-like state. For we are told in John 3 that “that which is born of the flesh is flesh; and that which is born of the spirit is spirit” (v.6); so in doing earthly things people of the world rely on their flesh; and when they can no longer use their flesh, it is time for their lives to end. Similarly, if a Christian cannot use his or her spirit, then that one must have fallen into a deep death-like state, so far as that believer’s spiritual walk is concerned.

Let us take note that the way Jesus quoted or referenced the Old Testament was different from the way the Pharisees did. And the explanation for this difference? Jesus had spirit whereas the Pharisees did not (see John 5:39-40). In spiritual things "similarity" is not a matter of unifying the doctrines; rather, it is an inward reality, for similarity is not identification and the difference between them is beyond the telling. For instance, one may imitate the voice, the tone and the teaching of another and obviously spiritual preacher; indeed, these stylistic and/or substantive traits in these two Christians may look and sound similar; but if there is no spirit accompanying the imitating preacher's ministry of God's word, these similar traits in him are but letters. The presence of the Holy Spirit in all things spiritual is the basis of true Christianity.

We are told in Matthew 7 that Jesus declared the following: "Many will say to me in that day, Lord, Lord, did we not prophesy by thy name, and by thy name cast out demons, and by thy name do many mighty works? And then will I profess unto them, I never knew you: depart from me, ye that work iniquity" (vv.22-23). So we may be zealous in working for the Lord, we may be able to cast out demons and to do many great wonders; nevertheless, the fundamental question does not concern itself as to the *quantity* of the work but as to the *character* of the work: namely, has all this work and activity been accomplished by the flesh or by the spirit? Only what has touched spiritual sense has been born of God's Spirit and is accepted by Him. He who would serve God must exercise his spiritual sense.

Exercise Spiritual Sense

1. Must Be Born Again

Now for any of us to be able to exercise spiritual sense we first of all need to begin from new birth. Suppose you try explaining to a born-blind person what is white color and what is red color by describing whiteness and redness to him. I believe that that blind person will most likely not be able to understand. Even if he be very, very intelligent, he nonetheless will probably still not be able to reason out the matter of colors; for cleverness of mind and having an understanding of colors one from the other are totally different talents in the world.

Jesus on one occasion asserted that "except one be born anew, he cannot see the kingdom of God" (John 3:3). What He meant by this was that new birth in a person's spirit is necessary for anyone to understand God's kingdom and other spiritual matters. These spiritual things cannot be understood by the carnal or unspiritual man. Only through spiritual sense can such things be known. And one's spiritual sense can only arise from new birth, for after a person is born anew God plants spiritual sense in that one.

2. Thorough Consecration

Secondly, we must have thorough consecration. This is what Romans 12 tells us. After we have presented ourselves as a living sacrifice, there will be the renewing of our minds, we thus being able to prove, discover or understand the will of God (vv.1-2). However, there are those in the church who have truly been saved and saved for many years but to whom if you speak about spiritual things their response ends up being like stone or wood towards such matters. This is because they have no spiritual sense at all, and that is mostly due to there being a problem with their consecration.

On the other hand, there are others in the church whose spiritual sense has suddenly been activated. And if the reason for this should be traced, the source for such is usually to be found in those believers' thorough consecration. Usually, though not always, a Christian's consecration is supplementary—that is, it is chronologically subsequent—to new birth. Prior to their consecration such Christians may have been very knowledgeable about such earthly interests as music, government, philosophy, and so forth; but if you spoke to them regarding spiritual matters, they exhibited no understanding. This is because only the spiritual—those having spiritual sense—can know the things of God, and that only by the Spirit of God. Earthly wisdom and cleverness cannot know the things of the Spirit of God (see I Corinthians 2:8-14).

The word translated in English as mind in Romans 12:2 is the Greek word *nous* in the original. Its better English translation is the word understanding. Formerly our spirit was dead, but by new birth it has now been made alive by the Holy Spirit; and thus our spirit has been enabled to communicate with God. However, we still need the renewal of our mind or understanding in order that we may know or understand on a daily basis what is the good and perfect and acceptable will of God. Hence, the understanding of our mind needs to be renewed often.

What, then, is the reason the spiritual sense in many Christians is dull or even non-existent? It is due to the lack of the renewal of their minds; and the reason for such lack of renewal is due to a flawed consecration. I have never witnessed a Christian whose consecration has been thorough having a dull spirit. Such a Christian lives out his life as a living sacrifice: the more thorough his or her consecration the more alert is that one's spiritual sense. This is because such consecration gives the Holy Spirit His rightful place in the church. But should our consecration be flawed in any way, the Spirit's rightful place in the church will be hindered. Thorough consecration is therefore absolutely necessary to prevent passive resistance on the believer's part.

3. Exercise New Spiritual Senses

Now upon experiencing the renewal of our minds, we still need to exercise our spirits in order to gain spiritual sense. The last verse of Hebrews 5 tells us that we are to have our senses exercised to discern good and evil. In this instance, to exercise means one should follow the feeling or sense of the Holy Spirit. So, Romans 12:2 speaks of the renewal of the mind, whereas Hebrews 5:14 emphasizes the exercise of our spiritual senses; that is, we need to learn to react more to the feelings or senses of the Holy Spirit in our spirits. This can be likened to the experience of a child growing up, in that throughout the various stages of physical and psychological growth he learns to react differently according to the different situations with which he is confronted as he grows older. And if later the child, now a young man of twenty, should learn well concerning the direction of his thought and action, then by the time he is forty he may be considered to be a matured person.

Likewise, after new birth in Christ, brethren should learn well by starting early in their Christian walk to exercise their spiritual senses so as to know what is being forbidden by the Holy Spirit, what is His leading, and what is not His leading. And if you nonetheless remain ignorant of these spiritual sensings of the Holy Spirit in your spirit, then you are an immature child of God, possessing the sense of a ten-year-old in the Lord when you are actually one who has been a believer for forty years (cf. Hebrews 5:11-14).

We Christians are different from worldly people after our new birth in Christ. We cannot any longer use the senses we learned to exercise in the flesh as we were growing up; instead, we need to develop and exercise new senses after our new birth. For instance, a blind person has his own senses as one who is physically blind. But if his eyes be opened to see, he gains a new set of senses. Even so, after new birth we Christians gain a new and different set of senses. But if we do not exercise our new senses, we will not be able to help others to know spiritual sense. Many things are hard to explain; they must therefore be learned. Unless we learn well, we will fail to know when our senses are telling us that our thoughts or actions/reactions are wrong or incorrect. Indeed, it will not be unlike the physically blind, in that due to their inability to exercise any sense of eyesight, all colors appear to them to be, incorrectly, all black. Hence, the necessity that we Christians exercise our new set of senses—all of which are spiritual, and not fleshly, in nature.

Therefore, we must ask the Lord to help us to maintain our consecration. This is an act of worship (Romans 12:1c mgn) which we must continually exercise throughout our Christian walk. None of us can say that he or she has graduated from consecration. We must keep our consecration freshly activated throughout life, and we must also exercise our senses to touch the spiritual instead of using our thoughts. The physically blind pay much attention to their hearing, using their ears for sounds as an aid to engaging in their daily activities as compensation for their lack of eyesight. But once their eyes are opened, they automatically cease depending upon their hearing faculty and now wish fervently to see more and more of the heretofore closed view of the world around them. Similarly, we Christians, prior to our salvation, paid great attention to our strong mind, emotion and will, utilizing them much. But after experiencing our spiritual rebirth, we are no longer to rely upon our wandering thoughts, old feelings and weak will in knowing how to pursue our walk and work before God. We must instead exercise our spirits more and more and follow our spiritual senses.*

* Note: Message given on 27 February 1950.

CHAPTER NINE
SPIRITUAL SENSE (CONCL'D)

"And Jehovah God formed man of the dust of the ground, and breathed into his nostrils the breath of life; and man became a living soul" (Genesis 2:7).

"A new heart also will I give you, and a new spirit will I put within you; and I will take away the stony heart out of your flesh, and I will give you a heart of flesh. And I will put my Spirit within you, and cause you to walk in my statutes, and ye shall keep mine ordinances, and do them" (Ezekiel 36: 26-27).

"But he [Jesus] turned and rebuked them, and said, Ye know not what manner of spirit ye are of" (Luke 9:55 mgn).

"That which is born of the flesh is flesh; and that which is born of the Spirit is spirit" (John 3:6).

"But the hour cometh, and now is, when the true worshippers shall worship the Father in spirit and truth: for such doth the Father seek to be his worshippers. God is spirit: and they that worship him must worship in spirit and truth" (John 4:23-24 mgn).

"It is the Spirit which quickens, the flesh profits nothing: the words which I have spoken unto you are spirit and are life" (John 6:63 Darby).

"But now we have been discharged from the law, having died to that wherein we were held; so that we serve in newness of the spirit, and not in oldness of the letter" (Romans 7:6).

"For we are the circumcision, who worship by the Spirit of God, and glory in Christ Jesus, and have no confidence in the flesh" (Philippian 3:3).

"For I know that this shall turn out to my salvation, through your supplication and the supply of the Spirit of Jesus Christ" (Philippians 1:19).

"If we live by the Spirit, by the Spirit let us also walk" (Galatians 5:25).

The Way to Communicate with God

Today I wish to speak of spiritual senses and how to walk after the Spirit. Any sensation in our spirit comes from the Holy Spirit having first moved in our spirit. But thought does not need the Holy Spirit in us to stir itself up first for it senses from using our mind. Our fellowship with God as Christians depends on our spirit. For God's Spirit dwells in our spirit. By our spirit we sense God's movement. Thus we are able to communicate with Him, to know Him and His will. As I indicated yesterday, before we were saved we had the habit of using our mind for the daily direction of our lives in the world. If after our salvation, however, we still depend on the mind instead of the movement of the Holy Spirit in our spirit, we are seriously wrong. If for years we Christians have failed to learn to follow the Holy Spirit, we will not be able to discern His movement nor will we know the place of our renewed mind in our spiritual sensing. It is when the Spirit moves in us, and we sense Him in our spirit that we then begin to use our mind to interpret His feeling in our spirit. Otherwise, the entire exercise will prove useless if we continue to think our own thought while the Holy Spirit is stirring in us.

How often we assume that if an individual is born with a clever, sharper mind, that person will be able to more quickly discern and understand the things of God than if he or she were born with a dull mind. Yet God's word does not confirm this notion. For He has said: "I will destroy the wisdom of the wise, and the discernment of the discerning will I bring to nought" (I Corinthians 1:19). God places the wise and foolish on the same footing. Neither the world's clever mind or foolish mind has any worth before God; everyone needs to be renewed in mind. Furthermore, God does not need any to be His counselor: as the Scripture inquires, "Who hath been his counsellor?" (Romans 11:34b) God does things according to His will, not according to our human reasoning. He declared, "Jacob I loved, but Esau I hated" (Romans 9:13). Again, He announced: "I will have mercy on whom I have mercy, and I will have compassion on whom I have compassion" (v.15).

Hence, God acts according to His will, not according to human reason, viewpoint or even sense of justice. If we follow God on the basis of viewpoint, reason and human justice, we will be forcing Him to follow our mind's approach to things. But we are God's bondmen, as lowly as the dust particles of the earth. We can only prostrate before His throne void of any argument with him.

We have no other way to live as Christians but to obey and follow the leading of the Holy Spirit in us. We can only stand on the ground of obedience. We cannot interfere with God and act as His counselor. Our mind can only reason and consider, but God does not want us to reason with Him; instead, He asks us to obey His will. A person may argue with his friend, but an aged father has no need to argue with his children of three or five years old. Our God is far above us—in fact, the distance between Him and us is immeasurable in every way. No one can approach His glory, for if He should reveal just a little of His glory to us, we would instantly prostrate before Him, casting away all reasoning. Therefore, let us follow God not in mind but in spirit.

Our Renewed Spirit: the Organ in Us to Know God's Will

Before proceeding further, let me briefly review what has previously been pointed out already. The organ in us by which to know God's will is the spirit, for it alone can contact God and know Him. The faculty of the mind is not able to know God. Should we use our mind, we will not be able to contact Him, nor can we sense the Holy Spirit. Our spiritual organ alone may contact God and sense Him.

Hence, in this regard the mind is totally useless. The reason why we believers in Christ may know the things of God is because He has given us a new spirit when we were saved (see Ezekiel 36:26), enabling us to sense and touch His Spirit whom He has given us for the purpose of revealing the things of God to us. Indeed, I Corinthians 2:11-12 informs us that apart from the Spirit of God no one may know the things of God.

The Holy Spirit in us gives senses to our spirit, thus causing us to know whether to walk quickly or slowly or not to walk at all. By exercising these spiritual senses, we may know what to do in pursuing and living out our Christian life rightly. This entire spiritual process can be likened to a horse on which has been placed a bit and bridle that will enable the horseman to control and direct the horse's every movement and action. By knowing these controlling senses the horse is able to conduct itself according to the desire and direction of the rider on its back: whether to move quickly or slowly, go forward or backward, turn left or right, or remain motionless. By pulling, relaxing, lifting or lowering the bit and bridle the rider can manage the horse according to his wishes. In like manner, the Holy Spirit will continually be giving us inwardly a variety of spiritual senses in our spirit which are meant to indicate God's will and wish for us in this, that or the other situation or circumstance of life or service. When, for example, we are exaggerating in our speech, the Spirit in our spirit will instantly bring this incorrect behavior to our attention; or when we are too talkative, He will let us know to cease.

I can recall one particular Christian brother who, before he was saved, often boasted that he was always the soul of every festive gathering. After experiencing the Lord's salvation, however, he soon thereafter was no longer the center of attraction. For having now become a Christian, whenever he spoke too much at a feast, he would feel uneasy about it after arriving back home. It had formerly been the case that the more the gathered people would hear him talk the greater in himself he felt. But now he felt otherwise and soon ceased being the center of attraction. This is a very good example of the guidance of the Holy Spirit in providing spiritual sense to the believer.

Suppose you sense you should preach the gospel to a certain person. The Holy Spirit has prompted and notified you and has thus given you sense in your spirit. If you follow His leading and do it, you experience peace and joy afterwards. For us to live and serve according to the Holy Spirit is to follow His movement in us. If we know and recognize the stirrings in our spirit as they are given by the Holy Spirit, we may walk after the Spirit.

Exercise Our New Spiritual Senses

All we who are saved have spiritual senses, but we must exercise them. As was pointed out previously, people who are born blind are very dependent upon their fingers and ears. But when their blind eyes are opened and they begin to see for themselves the many things in the world, they soon learn not to depend any longer upon their senses of touch and hearing for their visual sense. Likewise, after we are saved, with our spiritual sense having been restored, we henceforth must learn not to depend upon our other senses—such as mind, will or emotions—in the place of our new spiritual senses.

Let us examine this point further, once more using the blind to illustrate the matter. A blind person has no way to actually see the beauty of the gold edge of the pages in some Bibles. He can touch the edges of the Bible's pages but he cannot see, sense or recognize the gold-tinted edge. It is because the hand cannot substitute the eye. Similarly, the mind cannot substitute the leading of the Holy Spirit in our spirit. If today a blind man has his sight restored, he may still unnecessarily rely upon his old sense of touch by which to know things. So though he now has the new faculty of seeing, he must begin to exercise it. In the same way, many Christians after their salvation do not exercise their newly restored spiritual sense which God has given them but continue to rely upon their old sense of mind or feeling; and hence, they remain ignorant of the things of God.

It would be laughable were the eyes of a blind person to be opened and the person not use them. During the years of blindness he could only use the sense or faculty of touch upon a Bible by which to know its shape. But with his sight restored he is able to see the Bible and know its shape directly. In like manner, prior to an individual's salvation, a person might use his thought and reasoning powers in an attempt to know God and His will (cf. Acts 17:27). But once the person is saved and given a new spirit, he should no longer employ the faculty of the mind by which to know God and the way of the Holy Spirit. For this would be like the formerly-blind-but-now-seeing-person continuing to use the sense of touch and not that of sight by which to discern what color is the cover of a particular Bible.

Unless we use the organ of our spirit we are unable to distinguish many spiritual things, for the Holy Spirit guides us through our new spirit. Hence, unless we use our spirit we have no way of receiving whatever message is sent by the Holy Spirit nor of moving according to His leading.

John 3:6 intimates that as soon as we are born again we receive a new spirit through the Holy Spirit. And John 4:24 continues by saying that God is spirit, therefore, we must worship Him in spirit. Within our new spirit there is the Holy Spirit himself. The Spirit in God dwells in us today. As soon as the Holy Spirit in God moves, the Holy Spirit in us also moves; and this move touches our spirit, causing our spirit to know and to move and act accordingly. Thus we may begin to learn how to fellowship with God through our spiritual sense.

For example, if one born blind has his eyes opened when he is thirty years old, his eyesight is nonetheless only as old as a kindergarten pupil. Now a good set of eyes in a person may be able to see over a distance of perhaps two hundred miles whereas one's hands can at most touch objects within a distance of two or three feet. So unless this formerly blind person exercises his restored eyesight, his contact with the world will be forever limited to what his hands had enabled him to have during his blind period if, now that he is able to see, he were to continue to rely only upon the use of his hands by which to know the world around him. Let us now, however, apply this analogy spiritually to the Christian. Suppose that a fifty-year-old Christian has just been newly born in Christ. His spiritual eye or sense is obviously but one day old, whereas his physical eyesight is of course fifty years old. Yet, if during a period of fifty years following his new birth his spirit will have been continuously exercised in sensing spiritual feelings in knowing God and His will, then his spiritual eye or sense would be a mature fifty years old. Otherwise, he would remain a babe spiritually so far as his spiritual sense were concerned.

It is said in Hebrews 5:12-14 that according to exercise some believers should be teachers, yet they remain as babes. This is indicative of the fact that our spiritual sense must grow through exercise (v.14). The foundation of our Christian faith is having spiritual sense. Should we Christians always use our thought, reasoning and memory instead of our spirit, we shall forever be a stranger to spiritual things and shall remain as babes in spirit.

The Function of the Mind

Perhaps some will ask, Where, then, is the use of the mind? It is to be clearly understood that I do not say here that mind has no use. On the contrary, the function of the mind is much related to that of the spirit. For God communicates with us in our spirit; but it is also through our mind. How is the function of the elements of the soul—in this case, the mind—connected with the function of the spirit? The mind is the faculty in redeemed man by which to *understand* spiritual sense. Yes, with our open spirit, we may freely communicate with God. But to understand the leading in our spirit by the Holy Spirit, we have to use our mind. For instance, after a blind person's eyes are opened, he still uses his ears and hands, yet he now learns to use them in coordination with his eyes. Thus, though before being saved a person lived a life very much in and of the mind, he still uses his mind after his salvation, but only in coordination with his spirit.

To return again to the analogy of the blind man, once his eyesight has been restored, he will use his eyes whenever needed, unlike in his former blindness he had used his hands to touch and his ears to hear to compensate for the inability to use his blind eyes. But he must now also learn to coordinate the other senses of his body—such as touch and hearing—with his restored eyesight. Similarly, in the spiritual realm, after we Christians are saved, we must no longer use the mind in the *first* instance when it comes to the matter of spiritually seeing or sensing in our spirit the movement of the Holy Spirit. Rather, once the spirit has received the Spirit's leading, we must then coordinate our renewed mind with our spirit by the mind providing an understanding or explanation of what our spirit has received. That is why Paul wrote that we not only need the spirit's sensing but also the understanding of the mind (see I Corinthians 14:14-19).

Now how do we use our renewed mind? I would like for us to consider three particular workings of the mind.

First: Interpreting the Holy Spirit's Movement in Our Spirit

The words of I John 3:24, Romans 8:9 and I Corinthians 2:12 all mention the fact of God's Holy Spirit dwelling in our spirit. These are references to the divine outpouring of God. Having the Holy Spirit dwelling in us enables us to be connected to God. For He dwells in God as well as in our spirit. For us to say that the Holy Spirit is our spirit is not far off the mark for He dwells in us. But in saying that He is God's Spirit is absolutely right for the Holy Spirit is God. Hence this is why, when the word spirit is alone mentioned in the epistles, sometimes it is not clearly discernible whether it refers to the Holy Spirit or the human spirit. It is truly difficult to determine. This is due to the fact that the Holy Spirit of God dwells in man's spirit.

Because of this close intimate connection between the two, therefore, whenever the Spirit of God moves in my spirit, the latter will immediately sense it, whereas the mind of my outward man knows nothing of it. That is why I must use my mind to interpret to myself the meaning of the Spirit's movement in me. For instance, as you are actively engaged in doing a certain activity you begin to sense in your spirit that God by His Spirit is making a stir there. Nevertheless, though your spirit has been stirred, it will only be after your mind has interpreted or explained the meaning of the inward spiritual movement or stirring that you come to know that you are to continue or cease the activity. Such is the working of the mind.

This same working of the mind will be evident in our talking with someone about something. For instance, let us say that you are asking someone to accompany you in going somewhere. And suppose at one point in your conversation with the other party that your spirit stirs within you and your mind immediately interprets the meaning of the inward stirring, enabling you to know that you should not go forward with your intention because the mind has explained the stirring as being a forbiddance by the Holy Spirit to go there. You therefore even cease asking the other person to accompany you.

Hence, the work of the mind is to make it possible for us to understand the sensation given by God's Spirit in our spirit. We may thus define this task of the mind as the work of interpretation so that our outward man—our soul—may know what God by His Spirit in our spirit is telling us is His will for us at a given moment in a given situation or circumstance in our walk and service before God.

Second: Helping in Ministering God's Word

The second work of the mind is to help in the ministry of God's word. For example, suppose you sense in your spirit that God wishes you to speak on consecration. But after prayer and reading the Scriptures you have no anointing nor do you have any words. So, you do not pursue anything further along that message line. Later, however, you feel moved that you should speak on faith. At that moment you begin to sense light, and also words for delivering such a message commence coming to you. Moreover, your spirit responds positively and all things seem right. And upon arriving at the meeting you are not only able to speak on faith according to your spiritual sense but are also able to speak with the words which your mind, having been exercised, has given you. First, therefore, you must learn the right leading from God by His Spirit's movement in your spirit, then with the mind choose just those words God would have you to say, and, finally, deliver the word of God for that particular occasion. And as you are speaking forth the message on faith, the Holy Spirit within you will either keep indicating you are to continue speaking or else give you a spiritual sense within that you should bring the message to a conclusion.

Third: Helping to Know the Holy Spirit's Guidance in Our Daily Life

In our daily life we need to follow the guidance of the Spirit of God. Our mind can help us to know the guidance of the Holy Spirit in our daily walk. Consider, for instance, the kind of experience any one of us might be confronted with out in the world and which requires the assistance of our mind. Let us say, then, that yesterday you witnessed a thief stealing from your next-door neighbor's home. Today a police officer invites you to go over to your neighbor's home and shows you many photos of various thieves. As you examine them, you single out one of the photos as being that of the person you saw yesterday committing the robbery. Singling out this particular thief's photo is because you have more of his image in your mind's eye than you do regarding any of the other thieves' photos shown you.

Now spiritually speaking, the way our mind and spirit work together is similar to this example from the world. When the thought of our mind and the sense of our spirit agree, our spirit has sensed correctly. At times we may put forth many points from our mind for us to consider, yet our spirit might not be in agreement with them. On the other hand, on another occasion we may only raise a few points in our mind, and in this instance our spirit may immediately respond positively. So we must train our mind to such an extent that the moment a point in our mind is touched, our spirit will respond instantly with an amen.

Such is the working of mind and spirit together within the individual Christian. However, let us consider this same process of agreement or non-agreement within the context of Christians laboring together in serving the Lord. People often wonder why it is when each of them might be working with another believer in serving God, that that other person turns out to be always right but they themselves are always wrong. If I am asked this, my answer would be as follows: You have right reason in your mind, all right, but the inward spirit in the other person cannot offer an amen in agreement. We who serve God with others ought not to be looking to determine whether a person's reason is right or wrong but instead should look to see if our spirit can amen that other person's mind or not.

Read the Bible and Listen to Preaching with the Spirit

We will now see in what manner we must read the Bible and listen to preaching. In both cases there are two ways: one is to use the mind and the other is to use the spirit. If we read the Bible with our mind without using our spirit, the words of Scripture turn to be mere letters. It is not unlike having a body that without life becomes a corpse. We may know the Bible's teachings and doctrines by using our mind, but without the Holy Spirit's revelation we have no life (cf. John 5:39-40). Just as the Holy Spirit is in God so also is the Spirit in the word of God (see John 6:63 Darby, II Timothy 3:16 mgn, II Peter 1:20-21).

Therefore, should a sentence in the Bible lack the Spirit of God behind it, it is not God's word. The challenge for the Christian today is: the Holy Spirit has two kinds of word: the outer word of letter and the inner word of the Spirit. The challenge is to discern or know which kind of word you are touching in your approach to the Holy Scriptures.

Today, there is spirit in us as well as there is the Spirit in the Bible. If in our approach to the Scriptures we fail to use our spirit, it will be our outward man—our soul—that is in touch with the physical Bible and its text. We have not touched the Spirit in the Bible. Jesus once declared: "A prophet is not without honor, save in his own country, and in his own house" (Matthew 13:57b). This is because that prophet's countrymen only know his background and lifestyle, and thus they know the man only after his outward form and not according to his inner spirit as well. If you read the Bible solely according to its outward form, all you will acquire is doctrines, teachings and factual knowledge. You have not touched the Spirit of God's word.

Let our spirit be always hungry as we prepare to study the Bible, then we will receive the supply of life from God's word. For the Bible has two kinds of words: one kind are the words written in black letters on white paper; the other are words which have life for my spirit; that is to say, the kind of words which gives life to my spirit and thus satisfies my inward need for a powerful spiritual supply. Consequently, in reading the Bible we must not merely touch the doctrines, teachings and factual knowledge therein but we must also receive a needful supply in our inner spirit (cf. Philippians 1:19).

The same is true with respect to our hearing God's word preached. If in listening to the preaching of Holy Writ you only sense the preacher's eloquence, clear mind and good presentation, what you end up gaining are merely knowledge and doctrine. For you to receive spiritual supply from a preacher's words you must use your spirit to touch the spirit behind his words. Then you will be helped by his word by receiving the supply of his spirit (cf. again Philippians 1:19).

In listening to the Bible being preached we must use our spirit more than our mind. Just as a young bird opens its mouth wide to receive food from its mother so we must open wide our spirits in order that by the time the church meeting has concluded we will have gained strength and have satisfaction in our spirits. If the spirits of brothers and sisters are open wide, then they will be able to discern whether or not the preacher has used his spirit. Loud voice and incisive words are not necessarily signs or indications of using one's spirit while preaching. On the contrary, such an indication is not determined by loud voice, eloquence or sharp reasoning but whether or not one's preaching has drawn echoes of agreement from the spirits of the listening brethren and has given spiritual supply to their innermost being. A preacher's mind may deceive, but his spirit cannot. Some Christians may preach beautifully from beginning to end, yet they may not necessarily be in spirit while doing so. Having spirit or not is clear.

Speaking, Preaching, and Living According to the Spirit

Now just as we must exercise our spirit in reading the Bible or listening to preaching, so in every other aspect of our daily spiritual life we must make sure we act from the spirit. The temptation among young people in the Lord is to emphasize reasoning and neglect their spirit. Mankind's original fall while being tempted was essentially caused by neglecting the exercise of spirit in favor of the exercise of mind. Once a young man inquired of me: "I have studied theology for eight years and besides that I study the Bible more than ten hours daily. Why is it, then, that I have not received light?" My explanation was simply this: "You mistakenly think that if you spend time studying the Bible with your mind you will receive light. Not so. Only the spiritual—by which is meant those who exercise their spirit—can understand the things of God, even as the Scriptures have told us in I Corinthians (2:11-12,14). The same is true for anyone who seeks to minister God's word: it is the preacher who uses his spirit who shall receive light and revelation. In every aspect of our spiritual life we must use spirit more than mind."

One may outwardly speak humbly but he may not necessarily be a humble person. The truly humble, however, will always speak humbly. Similarly, one may deliver what appears to be spiritual speech, nevertheless, he is not necessarily being spiritual; but the spiritual person will only speak spiritually. A preacher must preach in the Holy Spirit. Now in the case of some preachers the Holy Spirit is willing to cooperate, whereas with others He refuses to cooperate. In order for you to preach in the Holy Spirit you need to be a spiritual person who uses spirit. Some while preaching may be unclear in words and poor in grammar, but because there is the presence of spirit in them, the Holy Spirit could launch out to change people in the audience. It is wrong for some preachers to attempt to substitute eloquence in speech for the spirit; it will be ineffective.

The quality of some people's spirit is right and dependable. Such is of sterling quality. But that of others may be quite low. The *words* of our brother Mr. T. Austin-Sparks cannot be compared with his *spirit*, for his spirit is of a very high quality. Once you have heard his prayer, you would agree and sense that his spirit has been released in a high, clear and pure manner. What we should all therefore seek after is a pure and strong spirit. Yes, indeed, some people may have a clean spirit yet it is weak. In my experience as a Christian I have been fortunate to have had the opportunity to sense in the prayers of sister Margaret Barber as well as in those of brother Austin-Sparks that their spirits are strong and pure. Young people should ask themselves if their words have spirit and are strong and pure. If not, they should begin to learn. All brothers and sisters must exercise their spirits.

Final Words

In order for a person to have quick spiritual sense and move according to the spirit, there are three requirements which must be present in that one. First, there must be genuine regeneration. Second, there must be thorough consecration. And third, there must be spiritual exercise. By possessing these three essentials your spiritual sense will advance greatly after a mere three months. As you work in service together with others, what is more important than even to finish a given work is for you to pursue after the spirit. Let us learn not to undertake any service for the Lord apart from the spirit. As you begin to do something you first must ask are you in the spirit or have you left the spirit? As you sing or pray or testify, these must be done in the spirit. Otherwise, you may harm the spirit of the brethren.

It is not a question of whether you open your mouth to speak to or for God, but whether you have followed the spirit in doing so. It is wrong to open your mouth without using your spirit. I am not here persuading you to open or close your mouth but simply to persuade you to follow the spirit—to use your spirit and not quench the Holy Spirit.

As you learn to exercise in this matter, your spiritual sense will be sharpened. And if that be the case with all brethren, God will be able to accomplish great things in the church.*

* Note: Message given on 28 February 1950.

Chapter Ten
How to Make a Decision in the Church

Two Spiritual Principles in the Church

There are two spiritual principles in the church: the first one is authority, and opposite to it is submission. Without authority the church will be filled with the flesh and without authority the church will be full of laws as in a court. And the second spiritual principle is love, for love edifies.

Neither Democracy Nor Dictatorship

In order to have order and convenience all the organizations in the world have their rules and regulations. For the sake of order and convenience in spiritual affairs the church has her own way of doing things. Every brother and sister has a part in the affairs of the church. For so many to be involved in service there must be arrangement; otherwise, the situation will be chaotic. In deciding matters, the way of the world is by majority rule or dictatorship or else the way is for one or a few to decide. However, the way in church management cannot follow worldly ways. It must be done according to the revelation given by God in the Bible. We must learn to follow the way of decision as given therein. Unless the church uses the Biblical way of decision, it will either adopt outright the worldly methods or adapt them in some fashion.

Revelation chapters 2 and 3 mention seven churches, the last one being the church in Laodicea, which follows the mentioning of the church in Philadelphia. As we shall shortly see, the risen Lord's word to the last church is most severe. The English proper name translated as Laodicea is formed from the two Greek words *laos* and *dikeia. Laos* means people, especially people assembled, whereas *dikeia* has three different meanings: (1) custom, habit; (2) rights; and (3) request, judgment or revenge. Laodicea thus means people's custom, people's right, and people's decision. Its overall meaning can be said to be simply as: people's opinion. In Revelation 2 and 3, this word *laos* has been used three times: one time here, whereas the other two instances of its use are included in the proper Greek name *Nikolaitai* translated into English as Nicolaitans. This name is twice cited in Revelation 2, with its name in the Greek original being a combination of the two words *nikao* (meaning, to conquer) and, of course, *laos* (meaning people, especially, people assembled). Hence, the name *Nikolaitai* in English means: (those who) conquer the people.

These same two chapters tell us that the things which the Laodiceans and Nicolaitans did or stood for were hated or highly disliked by the Lord. If, therefore, the way of service in the church is marked either by a conquering or compromising attitude and conduct, such is greatly reproved by the Lord. Not even majority rule is to be tolerated. If majority rule is to be accepted, then Christ should indeed have been condemned and crucified (see Matthew 27:21-23). Nor is it to be considered right and acceptable by the Lord for one man or a few people together to make a decision in and for the church. That is what has developed in the Roman Catholic Church, wherein a pope alone, or in consultation with a few others at the Vatican in Rome, decides matters for that Church. Such an arrangement is but a form of Nicolaitan conduct and teaching.

The Example in Acts 15

How, then, should the church make decisions? Although God has not given us any specific instruction or direction, He has nonetheless shown us in the Bible an example of the church's decision-making procedure in the church conference that has been laid out for us in great detail in Acts 15. The conference described there was spiritual in character, not earthly or worldly. It was conducted neither in terms of dictatorship nor majoritarian democratic rule. As revealed in Acts 15 the church conducted herself in ways of consultation and final decision-making that had this conference record not been included by Luke in his Acts narrative, we would be at a great loss today in knowing how to manage church affairs.

Before proceeding further it will be helpful to focus briefly on the background which lay behind the convoking of this Jerusalem church conference that is recorded for us in Acts 15. The church in Jerusalem could be considered as having been a senior church back then, for Christ had labored there and the twelve apostles had also spent much time there. Even the gospel had initially been spread by the Christians in Jerusalem who later had then spread it abroad, they having been scattered elsewhere from Jerusalem because of a great persecution which had broken out against this church (Acts 8:1b). Years later when Paul and Barnabas had returned to their home church at Antioch in Syria after their first missionary trip, they encountered great difficulty there. For some believers coming from Jerusalem to Antioch had been teaching the brethren that believers in Christ must be circumcised according to the regulations of Moses. Unless they were circumcised, for example, they were not saved.

Paul and Barnabas argued heatedly with them. These two apostles were clear that if after believing in Christ we are not justified and were therefore still unredeemed sinners, then Christ had died for nothing (see Galatians 2:17-21). Hence, it was their view that the church must never confuse or mix up salvation with various elements of Judaism such as circumcision, Sabbath, eating regulations, and so forth. Otherwise, in the future, people might arise and teach that unless a person has a college degree or becomes a vegetarian or meets some other peculiar requirement, that person is not saved. How different is the pure gospel, for it simply teaches that anyone who believes in the Lord Jesus is saved. Since, therefore, this teaching, which called for the keeping of the Mosaic law in order to be saved, had come to Antioch from Jerusalem, Paul and Barnabas went to Jerusalem for fellowship over this critical matter. Other brothers in the church at Antioch also went there with these two apostles.

1. Many Brothers Might Speak

After Paul and Barnabas arrived in Jerusalem, they did not initially seek out Peter. Instead, they went to see "the apostles and the elders" (Acts 15:2), and "they were received by the church and the apostles and the elders" (v.4). Then the apostles and the elders called all the brethren who were there to a meeting. We see from this that should anything of this serious a nature happen, the whole church should be called together for fellowship, with everyone having the privilege of speaking. The responsible brothers must listen to what the other brothers and sisters have to say.

Now even though the older brothers would be the ones who would ultimately make the decision, they would nonetheless listen to what the other brothers and sisters would like to say, for in the words of these other brethren there might come forth the voice of the Holy Spirit. Inasmuch as these older brothers had been greatly dealt with by the Lord, they would only make their decision before God after they had heard what the other brothers and sisters might say. In that same conference, however, there also stood up some believers who were of the sect of the Pharisees and who in their hearts believed differently, for they declared that "it is needful to circumcise them [the Gentiles], and to charge them to keep the law of Moses" (v.5). Thus there was much discussion. All this indicated that many brethren spoke in expressing their opinions.

2. Peter Spoke

"[After] much questioning" (v.7a)—which is to say that after all kinds of viewpoints had been voiced, Peter rose up in this church gathering and spoke. He related to them what had happened in the house of Cornelius at Caesarea. He pointed out the fact that it was not others who had first preached the gospel to the Gentiles but he himself, for "a good while ago God made choice among you, that by my mouth the Gentiles should hear the word of the gospel, and believe" (v.7b). What the apostle next said can readily be interpreted as him explaining the following: "We Jewish believers in Christ have had a deeply religious background, and as such, circumcision and keeping Sabbath are observances which for us were very easy to keep; but for the Gentile believers in Him, these will become a heavy yoke. We should therefore not place this heavy yoke upon their necks (see v.10)."

Now we may recall that in the house of the Roman centurion Cornelius all the Gentiles gathered there had (1) heard Peter preach the gospel, (2) received the gift of the Holy Spirit well before the apostle had finished speaking,

(3) believed on Jesus, and (4) only then had Peter commanded that they be baptized "in the name of Jesus Christ" (Acts 10:44-48). Indeed, from these Scripture verses we learn that it was *God* who had *acted first* by giving these Gentiles the Holy Spirit as a confirmation. And Peter later testified, as is recorded in Acts 11, that so far as concerned the *way* the Holy Spirit was given to these Gentiles at the centurion's home, it was the same as had happened "[to] us at the beginning" (v.15) in Jerusalem on the day of Pentecost: namely, we 120 believers in the Upper Room and these Gentiles at Caesarea were "baptized in [or, with] the Holy Spirit" (v.16b). On the other hand, so far as concerned the timing of *when* the Holy Spirit fell on Cornelius and his Gentile household, such had been just the reverse from the timing in Jerusalem on Pentecost outside the Upper Room; for on this earlier occasion at Jerusalem it was only after Peter had finished preaching the gospel and the three thousand newly-saved disciples had been baptized in water that they had received the promised gift of the Holy Spirit (Acts 2:38). If what had occurred with the Cornelius household had been in the same sequential order as had happened at Jerusalem on Pentecost day—that is, first water baptism and next receiving the Holy Spirit—then there would have been no amazement on the part of those Jewish circumcised believers who had accompanied Peter to the home of Cornelius (10:45). But as it happened, not long after the apostle began preaching to these assembled Gentiles, "the Holy Spirit fell on all them that heard the word" (Acts 10:44). This

thus demonstrated that it pleased the Holy Spirit to have done so prior to their water baptism. Whereas the Jewish believers of the party of the Pharisees, who, after this church conference had been opened up for discussion by the apostles and elders, spoke only of dead doctrine, Peter, when it was his turn to speak, spoke of the quickening work of the Holy Spirit.

3. Paul and Barnabas Spoke

After Peter finished speaking, all who attended the conference remained quiet. Then Paul and Barnabas followed by "rehearsing what signs and wonders God had wrought among the Gentiles through them" (15:12).

4. James Made the Final Decision

Finally, James rose up and spoke at some length (15:13-18). We are then told in verse 19 that James gave this conference the final decision. So at this church conference a first group of people spoke, giving the background; then the Jewish believers among the Pharisees spoke. Next spoke Peter. Next were Paul and Barnabas. And lastly, it was James who gave the final decision.

Today's Application of Acts 15

Today we may use this chapter's church meeting as an example for us to emulate. Decisions are not to be made based on the opinion of the many; rather, an opportunity must be provided for brothers and sisters to speak or debate at a church meeting. Before the final decision is made, all the brothers and sisters should be allowed to speak, a Peter or a Paul or a Barnabas can speak, and then a James speaks forth and makes the final decision.

The Rise of the Spiritual Leader in the Early Church

Our question today is: Who among us is a James? In other words, who is qualified to stand in the leading position and make a decision for the church? In order to answer this question, let us see how James became the leader back in those days, and then we may know how this spiritual leader was produced who could thus make such a church decision.

The Bible mentioned six people named James. The one who figured prominently at the church conference of Acts 15 was a brother of Jesus according to flesh. We learn from the New Testament that he spoke several times on several different occasions. Altogether, he was mentioned ten times in this part of the Bible. Now we know that at the beginning of the church the leader was Peter. It was he who led in the preaching of the gospel. Later on, it was Peter and John who went to Samaria to complete the work of the gospel begun there by the deacon-evangelist Philip (Acts 8:14). It was also Peter who went to the house of Cornelius (Acts 10). But after that time Peter seemed to lose his leadership in the church. Acts 12 tells us that the church was again greatly persecuted, with James an apostle having been killed and Peter having been imprisoned. At that time James the brother of Jesus appears to have emerged as a new leader whereas Peter seems to have lost his leadership position. Thus we notice from all this that spiritual leadership does not depend upon one's experience nor upon being elected to a leadership role as is the case in the election processes of the world. To the contrary, it depends upon who, before the Lord, has exhibited more spiritual exercise and progress, thus emerging into a leadership position.

We notice in First Corinthians 15:5-7 that Paul mentioned many people in a collective sense to whom the risen Lord had appeared; indeed, he only cites by name James and Peter. As for the rest, he merely refers to them as "the twelve," or "above five hundred brethren," or "all the apostles," and so forth; he did not even cite by name that of John the apostle. This would appear to indicate that besides Peter, James must be special, so Paul singled him out by name. Not just in this writing of Paul's but also in Galatians 1:18-19 Paul mentioned the names of only two apostles. And again they were Peter, and James the brother of the Lord—in that order. In Galatians 2:9, however, Paul, in writing of a later time, once more, when referring to those who "were reputed to be pillars [of the church in Jerusalem]," names James and Peter and John, in that order, as those from whom at Jerusalem he and Barnabas received "the right hands of fellowship"; thus at this time placing James ahead of Peter. And by the time of the subsequent events of 2:12ff., Paul tells his readers that "certain [brethren] came from James" to Antioch; he did not simply write that they came from Jerusalem. Moreover, immediately after Peter had been miraculously freed from prison by an angel of the Lord, Peter himself, we are told in Acts 12:17, said to his fellow believers that they were to "tell these things to James." At that time in Jerusalem there were quite a number of co-workers as well as tens of thousands of Christian brethren, yet Peter especially singled out James to be notified of his rescue from prison.

From all the foregoing verses we may readily discern that at the beginning of the church in Jerusalem Peter was the number one leader; but now we see that after he was imprisoned, James stood out as though ahead of Peter. This brief sketch of the rise of James to leadership in the church at Jerusalem explains how it was that he was the one who stood up at the last at that Acts 15 conference and made the final decision, for he had become the spiritual leader at that time.

The Spiritual Leader's Decision Is That of the Holy Spirit

We are told in Acts 15:19 that James made the decision, saying, "Wherefore, my judgment is" thus and so. Then these words of James are followed by the words of a letter, composed by the apostles and elders representing the whole church, that was to be carried to Antioch by Paul and Barnabas, along with the two Jerusalem church brothers, Judas and Silas: "... it seemed good to the Holy Spirit, and to us" (v.28a). We discern from all this that though the judgment originally pronounced was by James, it results in actually being the judgment of the Holy Spirit and the entire church. We may thus see that the judgment of the church's spiritual brethren is that of the Holy Spirit himself.

The Holy Spirit Alone Has Authority

From the Acts 15 narrative we come to realize that within the context of the fellowship of the entire church, all brothers and sisters may freely voice their opinions. Nevertheless, this does not signify that one's freely-voiced opinion must necessarily be followed. For as various brethren offer their opinions, the elders must listen carefully in order to detect and touch the voice of the Holy Spirit behind those brethren's voices. In fact, this spiritual exercise can be likened to what happened, as told of in Luke's Gospel, when the Virgin Mary visited her kinswoman Elizabeth, already six months pregnant with John the Baptizer: just as Elizabeth heard the voice of Mary greeting her, the babe in Elizabeth's womb leaped in response, and instantly she was filled with the Holy Spirit (1:44). The elders must be sensitive to hear the voice of the Holy Spirit in the speaking forth by the brothers and sisters. As the latter speak, their many and varied words may or may not be correct and their spirits may or may not be right. Hence, the listening elders must exercise their spiritual sense in discerning what is the voice of the Holy Spirit.

At times in a non-church discussion the voices can grow louder and increasingly emotional, and many will be the voices heard right up to the end. But with a church discussion, it will end in no voice being heard till the responsible brothers have come to a decision that will be final. They must use their spirits to touch and connect with the authority of the Holy Spirit in the church and then make the final decision. In such a process, therefore, the church—in coming to a decision—will not be following the opinion of the elders but the decision will be based on what the brothers and sisters have had to say as well as on the spirit of the prophet(s). Indeed, James' decision recorded in Acts 15 was not based on his personal opinion; instead, after he had heard what the brothers and sisters said, as well as having considered the spoken words of Peter, Paul and Barnabas, and, having been reminded by the Holy Spirit of the words of the Old Testament prophet Amos (9:11f.), James made the final decision (Acts 15:14-18).

Accordingly, the way of settling matters in the church is neither that of dictatorship nor committee-ship nor majoritarian democracy nor an oligarchy. The church does not make a decision by casting votes or by virtue of the decision of a few people. They are decided instead by the responsible brothers as guided by the leading of the Holy Spirit. Nevertheless, though there is neither democracy nor oligarchy nor one-man dictatorship in the church, those who are more spiritual will obviously emerge and advance to the foreground, whereas those who have learned less in both spiritual and practical experience before God will recede to the background. Even so, though those brothers who have learned more will assume leadership positions, they nonetheless do not in themselves have authority but must learn to let the Holy Spirit be the authority. We can notice this to some degree in the Scriptures: John was always behind Peter; James was behind Peter earlier but he later surpassed Peter. From the Gospel accounts we know that at first James did not believe in the Lord Jesus, but later on he ascended higher in spiritual leadership—in fact, much higher than the other Jewish believers in Jerusalem—just as Paul emerged higher spiritually among the Gentile believers.

Do please notice that in the Acts 15 account there was neither any so-called consultation among the church elders and/or apostles nor any deference towards the opinion of man nor the grounding of the final decision on any unspiritual or worldly considerations.

What is therefore required in the church is that brothers and sisters must learn to live humbly before God and express themselves humbly before their fellow brethren; and elders, prophets and apostles must be ever bright and alert in their spirits. It cannot be emphasized too much that the responsibility of the advanced brothers in the church is great. If anyone assumes a position of responsibility but fails to diligently learn spiritual lessons, the things of God will be destroyed in that person's hands. Hence, those in responsibility must, on the one hand, learn much in being dealt with by God, and, on the other hand, learn to follow the example of Acts 15 in listening to the voices of the brothers and sisters and in discerning the guidance and authority of the Holy Spirit.*

* Note: Message given on 1 March 1950.

CHAPTER ELEVEN
SPIRITUAL QUALITY

"And it came to pass, when the days were well-nigh come that he should be received up, he stedfastly set his face to go to Jerusalem, and sent messengers before his face: and they went, and entered into a village of the Samaritans, to make ready for him. And they did not receive him, because his face was as though he was going to Jerusalem. And when his disciples James and John saw this, they said, Lord, wilt thou that we bid fire to come down from heaven, and consume them? But he turned, and rebuked them, and said, Ye know not what manner of spirit ye are of. And they went to another village" (Luke 9:51-56 mgn).

Quality of Spirit: Contrast between Jesus and Two of His Disciples

Today I would like for us to consider together one important aspect to our Christian Life—that of spiritual quality. We mentioned a few days earlier that in our living, working or serving, we need to see if there is the spirit involved, as well as that we have spiritual sense. Today I want us to pay attention to the matter of spiritual quality. The words in Luke 9:51-56 have very much to do with spiritual quality. In this incident with the Samaritans

Jesus by His words of rebuke has revealed what kind of spirit the two disciples James and John had. From just a few verses earlier in Luke 9 we learn of the Lord Jesus having been transfigured on a mountain summit (vv.28-36). During that momentous event both the lawgiver Moses and the prophet Elijah were seen discussing with the Son of man the critical task He was soon to accomplish at Jerusalem. This indicates to us that God had already decided His will that Christ would be going to Jerusalem to accomplish the work of redemption for mankind. On the mountaintop, in fact, Jesus had himself decided the direction of His way and He now needed to be on His way. Hence, “He stedfastly set his face to go to Jerusalem” (v.51b).

On the way from the Mount of Transfiguration to Jerusalem, Jesus with His disciples would have to pass through many places, such as Jericho and a considerable number of towns and villages in the provincial area of Samaria. And as He would pass through each of these many Samaritan communities He would send people ahead to prepare His way. Now we know that the Samaritans did not have good feelings towards the Jews, whom they more often than not considered to be their enemies. So when they knew that Christ and His disciples had their faces set towards Jerusalem, they refused to receive the Lord and His party of travelers or to conduct any business relations with them.

When I was in London a decade or so ago, one day I was coming back from Southampton. It was quite late, so

I tried to find a hotel in which to spend the night. To my surprise the staffs of several hotels, recognizing that I was Chinese, refused me their services before I finally found one willing to take me in. On another occasion I happened to be in Chicago. It was at a time when an international exhibition was being held there. That day I encountered eight hotels which refused to accommodate me because I was a Chinese. But in contrast to my puny though unpleasant experiences of rejection, the Lord Jesus had set His face towards Jerusalem to be crucified for the sake of the gospel of redemption. What a tremendous purpose which lay behind His steadfast focus upon Jerusalem. Yet the Samaritans refused to entertain Jesus in the slightest manner. We shall notice how different His attitude was towards the rejective Samaritans, for following His resurrection the risen Lord had specifically instructed His disciples to preach His gospel of glad tidings not only in Jerusalem but also throughout all Judea *and* Samaria and from there to the ends of the earth (Acts 1:8b). Yet here at the very first community in Samaria the future Redeemer of mankind was being refused any welcome whatsoever.

The Lord Jesus, as we well know, was meekness and lowliness incarnate. So since the Samaritans would not receive Him, He did not remain there. Jesus could tolerate their refusal of himself, but the disciples could not. Hence, James and John wanted to demonstrate their affection for the Lord by doing that which they looked upon as being Scriptural—calling fire to fall from heaven by which to eliminate the Samaritans even as Elijah had as recorded in II Kings (1:9-12). For they had thought that here was a man who was greater than Elijah, and therefore, how could the Samaritans refuse to receive Him?!? Consequently, they besought the Lord to have Almighty God exhibit a testimony to men by having them see and understand that Jesus is the Christ whom He had established. Hence their zeal was not blindly expressed, for it did possess some basis in Scripture.

Yet the Lord turned and scolded these two disciples of His. Why? Let us clearly understand that Jesus was not blaming them here for their zeal according to Scripture; instead, He blamed them for their wrong spirit. What the Lord was indicating by His rebuke was that a person could very much love Him and act in fact according to the teaching and action of Scripture's Old Testament prophet and be quite zealous in doing so; nevertheless, his spirit might not be right. There was no question concerning the love and zeal of these Sons of Thunder towards Jesus, but the Lord, who knows human hearts, detected that their spirit was wrong. And because of this, Jesus could not hesitate to rebuke them. They were zealous in their love for the Lord, but their spirit was not right.

Must Have Right Spirit in Serving the Lord

So the question now is, What kind of spirit is right and what kind is wrong? In this passage of Scripture we learn that it is not enough for those who serve the Lord to have love and zeal only. They must also have the right kind of spirit. Whether or not one is acceptable to the Lord is not based on his behavior but on his spirit. The zeal, love and scriptural basis for action of these two disciples were all correct, yet their spirit was wrong; and thus, all which flowed out from their wrong spirit was not right and was therefore not praiseworthy. People of the world are praised for their seemingly good behavior, and even Christians are likewise praised—both within and without the church—according to their outward good behavior; nevertheless, they have already lowered their standard, since the Lord's standard for His followers is not right behavior but the quality of their spirit.

Although these two disciples were most zealous for the Lord, they were nonetheless blamable, for their spirit was wrong. What the Lord looks for is the condition of our spirit. What the world cares for are conduct, zeal and love; but the standard for the life of us Christians is the quality of our spirit. The issue is therefore centered upon the spirit and not upon matters of conduct. What many young people in the Lord strive for are Scriptural orthodoxy, zeal and love; the Lord, however, looks for but one thing: the quality of spirit.

Right Words vs Wrong Spirit

The Lord Jesus said that the disciples did not know the state of their spirit. Here we notice a curious facet to all this. Whereas James and John had proposed to the Lord that He have God send down consuming fire from heaven, Jesus did not rebuke them for speaking in this manner—as though He should blame them for their apparent wrong speaking; rather, Jesus rebuked them for their undeniably wrong spirit. In controversies which arise among brothers and sisters, I have often heard it remarked as to whose words were right and whose were wrong. My quarrel with controversies like this does not center around such a consideration. Brethren have frequently heard me observe that what so-and-so has said was not wrong but that so-and-so's spirit was wrong. We can discern from this incident with the Sons of Thunder that the Lord Jesus had not taken issue with the rightness or wrongness of their spoken words but with whether the spirit which lay behind their words was correct or not. This latter consideration is what the Lord always looks for preeminently. As soon as anyone opens the mouth, his or her spirit will come forth. And as one's spirit comes forth, it may or may not be right. Accordingly, we should look most importantly at the spirit and not at the words.

Know Your Spirit's Condition

Furthermore, Jesus' words here can also be interpreted as constituting a revelation to ourselves as to whether our spirits are wrong or not, since most likely we do not truly know ourselves. This was certainly true of these two disciples, who were overconfident in themselves; for they assumed that by simply adopting the words and action of Elijah they would be on solid ground scripturally in asking the Lord's permission—which in their minds He would readily grant—to bring judgment upon those inhospitable Samaritans. But they were totally ignorant of themselves and their wrong spirit.

Now it is no surprise that a person will sometimes have a wrong spirit; what may be surprising, however, is for a person to not know it. It is relatively easy to correct a wrong *act*; on the other hand, it is very difficult to restore a wrong spirit in a person who is totally unaware of it being wrong. The following two situations—one serious and one comical—provide clear parallels to this phenomenon. In the first one, the most frightening aspect which might be true about a given sinner's behavior would not be that the person has sinned but that the person does not know that he or she has sinned and that this sinner even prides himself or herself in having done a good deed when having sinned! It is hard to awaken someone who lies in such darkness. A second parallel situation is that of a child who, having gotten a blackened face, returns home unaware of it and when laughed at thinks such laughter is an indication of being liked by others! We should be fearful of having a wrong spirit and ourselves not be aware of it. Such a situation arises from a lack of revelation and light. As a person speaks, so is the state of that one's spirit. Yet often the condition of one's spirit is unknown to the person himself: "He that trusteth in his own heart is a fool," said Solomon (Proverbs 28:26a).

It is untrue to conclude that because people do not know they have a spirit, therefore they have no spirit. It is likewise untrue to conclude that because people do not know their spirits are wrong, therefore their spirits are not wrong. If a person's spirit is wrong, it is wrong. As people speak, their spirits are exposed. Jesus' two disciples were intent on vindicating the Lord, but His word of censure revealed that, first, they did not know their spirit; second, they did not know themselves; and third, they did not know that there was a wrong spirit in their spoken words. When you speak, you may not know the condition of your spirit, whether it is right or wrong. But some of your hearers may immediately know whether your spirit is right or wrong. They are those who have learned to recognize such instantly as they hear. The words spoken can be both scriptural and zealous in their presentation, but whether, first, there is spirit or not, and, second, whether there is a right or wrong spirit present, will be readily detected by those who have deeper fellowship with the Lord. I hope we may all learn before God. His standard for our Christian life is more than being Biblical, ethical and correct; our words and actions must be expressed in the right spirit.

Cultivating Good Quality of Spirit in Our Experience

Let us consider this matter from the viewpoint of experience. The human spirit is very special. According to the Scriptures man's spirit in and of itself has no quality. For it is above good or evil, right or wrong, and yea or nay. Spirit itself is a renewed ability given by God to the believer at new birth. The special feature of the spirit lies in its having no quality in itself but that its quality comes from elsewhere—even from the quality of the soul. As the self-life is added to the spirit there is character being produced in the spirit. So on the one hand, one may say that the spirit itself is truly without character, yet, on the other hand, were someone to say that the spirit *has* character, that would also be true, for its character follows the character of the outward man—the soul. Hence, the character of the spirit depends on that to which it is attached.

For example, water itself, if it is pure, has no color. But when added to it are various kinds of sugar, it will give off different colors and tastes. So is it with the Christian's renewed spirit: it is originally pure, but our spirit will take on whatever quality characterizes the kind of person we are in our soul. Oftentimes the words and the actions of our fellow brethren in Christ are correct but the accompanying spirit may not be right, for our outward man—even our soul- or self-life—may be wrong. Chapter 3 of John's Gospel says that our spirit must be born again. And its chapter 4 follows informing us that our worship of God must come from our spirit. So if our spirit is wrong, it cannot serve Him.

The famous evangelist, D.L. Moody, started out in his life as an apprentice to a shoemaker. And later as a beginning evangelist he had neither experience nor learning for such spiritual service. So when he first began to preach, his habit was to put various points together in the fashion of here a little, there a little. What points he had heard from others' sermons he would jot down and then use them in his own preaching. At an evangelistic meeting on one occasion some five or six hundred people stood up and expressed their faith in the Lord. But a middle-aged woman came to him after the meeting and criticized him for the grammatical and vocabular inaccuracy in his speech. As Moody listened to the woman his tears began falling down his cheeks and then he said to her: "You know me most, dear lady, you know me most; therefore, you should pray for me most." This woman was always criticizing people, and what she had told Moody was right but her spirit was wrong. Yet the opposite case was true of Moody: his preaching words might be wrong but his spirit was right. At that very time the ministry of Moody was at its height; nevertheless, he could be so humble as was the case on this occasion with this critical woman, for his humility came out of his life with the Lord. Some may appear to be humble, but such belongs to the soul and not the spirit. Moody was a man who was willing to have his soul dealt with. And as a consequence, this made his spirit clean. God could thus greatly use him.

At one time in Shanghai there was a Christian brother named Lee who did something wrong. Another brother, Chow by name, heard of it and was very concerned and sad. For a week he prayed earnestly, even fasting and shedding many tears. Then he went to brother Lee to persuade him with love, tears and a gentle spirit in an attempt to restore brother Lee, which resulted in his being convicted and showing repentance. However, it was merely an outward gesture, for brother Lee was not submissive inwardly. Two years later brother Chow committed the very same fault! When brother Lee heard of it, he immediately wrote a letter to brother Chow. In the letter there were but four short words of rebuke and nothing else: "Now how about you!" If the spirit of brother Lee had been right, there would not only have been words of blame expressed for the purpose of restoration but also tears of compassion. Yet here was a person who could advise people with four stern words of rebuke, but his spirit was wrong, even wicked. Now after brother Chow received the letter from brother Lee, he answered back immediately, saying: "Hence, we know that people are weak and can easily fall. Without the mercy and grace of the Lord, no one can stand. Therefore, you and I must fear God." Here in brother Chow we see a right spirit.

A right spirit comes from God, for we do not naturally possess it. When God speaks to us, we should submit instead of being self-righteous and proud; then at that point we shall have the right spirit. May we learn to open our spirits and accept God's Spirit. If anything from our soul-life that is impure is mixed in, the spirit will become unclean.

A certain St. Giles was a simple monk who at one time served as cook in a monastery in Italy north of

Rome during the Middle Ages.* He had had little formal education and possessed little learning in Bible knowledge during the early period of his life. People at that time looked with great favor upon learning, which thing Giles himself admired greatly. So one day he asked permission to attend some regular assemblies of the monks in order that he might hear the sermons. However, his request was turned down and he was ordered to remain in the kitchen.

Once when a special convocation of the year was approaching, he again requested permission to attend. Again his request was denied. Upon praying to the Lord about it, Giles felt there was a way of satisfying his desire to attend the gathering. Usually the bread was prepared daily and the food was also cooked every day just prior to serving every meal. But this time he prepared for two days' food supply by cooking in advance potatoes, duck meat, and so forth all together at one time, and putting this combined dish aside. Then, at meal time he simply heated it all up and served the monks. At the first meal of this kind the monks only sensed that the food was different in taste and appearance from the usual fare.

---

* This St. Giles (among several Catholic saints bearing that name) was possibly the one known as Blessed Giles of Assisi (d. 1262), who was a close friend of St. Francis of Assisi (1181/2-1226) and one of the earliest fellow members of the Catholic Franciscan order of lay monks founded by its famous namesake in about 1206 or 1207. The monastery in question was possibly one that was located in the town of Perugia north of Rome and Assisi itself.—*The Publishers*

But when the abbot of the monastery learned what had occurred, he scolded Giles severely. That night the humble cook was unable to sleep, but God enlightened him, causing him to know that all things occurring in his life had been permitted and/or arranged by Him. Instantly he saw where he had been wrong, and so he immediately repented.

Then he noticed that the abbot had come down with a sore throat. He felt badly about it. So he prepared a special oatmeal soup to be served with iced sugar cubes. He apologized to the abbot, saying the following: "Concerning the matter of the meals, I was wrong. Please forgive me. You have a sore throat. I have prepared this special soup for you." The abbot was greatly moved by this selfless and compassionate gesture, he having been touched by the self-giving spirit of Giles; and so he received a tremendous spiritual supply at the hands of the humble cook. Speaking naturally here, had I been in Giles's shoes I would have felt most unhappy at the abbot's scolding, but Giles did not harbor such feeling; instead, he was concerned about the abbot's health. He was willing to prepare food for the abbot even at midnight if necessary. Such a spirit as St. Giles exhibited was pure, and its quality was high.

We must inquire before the Lord as to whether or not we have spirit as well as quality of spirit. Throughout church history there have been many brothers and sisters who had an excellent spirit, well above what ordinary people would have. If we engage in spiritual exercise and frequently commune with God, it will be easy for the right spirit to come forth. Contrariwise, if we do not live constantly before God, an unclean spirit will come forth in our words. Whether our spirit is marked by good or bad quality depends upon our storing up before God in ordinary times the good quality in our spiritual reservoir.

Here I would like to speak for a few moments to the church elders present among us. In dealing with young people, I would urge you not to learn if they have wisdom, for human wisdom is useless. Neither should you deal with their gifts and usefulness. You must instead focus upon their spirit to see if it is clean or not. Whenever a problem arises among brothers and sisters, the issue of concern should not be that of who spoke first or who spoke later; neither should it be a matter of concern over procedure to be followed in the resolution of the problem; nor should it be concerned with who has had the right words or right conduct. What is most necessary is for you elders to focus upon their spirit.

If you accept at face value a young person's words, you elders do not really know whether or not their words are correct. If, further, you depend on the young people's behavior, they may have different standards. The secular courts look at facts and conduct; but church elders should not emphasize these. They should instead look at the condition of the young people's spirits.

To deal with young people, therefore, we must learn if they have a strong spirit or what exactly is its condition. Although young people may have strong spirits, their spirits may easily be contaminated or become wild and proud. May the Lord have mercy on those of us in leadership that we may lay emphasis more upon believers' spirits than upon their words and/or conduct.

In Serving God, There Needs to Be Spirit

Why is spirit necessary in serving God? This is because of the differing orders or levels of life which the Creator-God has established among all living beings on earth. As a consequence, it is extremely difficult for different levels or orders of life to have communication with each other. For instance, due to the order difference between lower and higher animals, it is well-nigh impossible for them to communicate with each other. Bird and insect, for example, may all fly, yet even here, their qualities of flying ability differ; and hence, because of the differing qualities inherent in their different levels or orders of life, they, too, cannot communicate with each other. Not even with differing orders of life that possess better qualities can there be communication. A dog, for example, has a keen smell, far keener than that of us humans; yet not because of that can it communicate with man, for its order of life is different. We may use a dog to guard our door or search for lost articles or even for lost or missing people, but we cannot communicate with a dog about human household affairs or human personal feelings.

Let us consider for a moment brother Yu's dog, which is called Tido. It has a given name but no surname. You cannot add a surname to its given name and call it Tido Yu, simply because it has no order-of-life relationship with brother Yu. The lack of communication between these two therefore lies not in its being a good or bad dog but because it is of a different order of life from that of man. So however clever brother Yu's dog may be, it cannot be called Tido Yu because its and brother Yu's life levels are different from each other. But with respect to brother Yu's *son*, no matter how foolish he may be, he is still brother Yu's son because he has the same order of life as that of his father. Then, too, whereas man uses the soul as his chief mode or life-source for living, God requires spirit as His means of living. God is the highest order of life. Man, even with his greater wisdom than that of animals, cannot by the mind of his soul communicate with God.

John 4:24 clearly says that God is Spirit, and that all who worship Him must worship in spirit and truth. Thus, all who worship God must employ the same quality of spirit to do so. For instance, though the loveliness of your dog and the loveliness of your son cause you to love them both, the quality of your love for your son is different from the quality of your love for your dog. Many unbelievers have presumed to believe that religion is a matter of emotion; but John 4 tells us that we cannot serve God with emotion but can only serve Him in and with spirit. Not only emotion is insufficient, even thought or wisdom is equally useless. All who depend exclusively on their soul cannot serve God; only with the spirit may we serve Him.

We need to pay special attention here to John chapters 3 and 4. These two serve as two very important pillars of spiritual truth in the Bible. From chapter 4 we learn that God is Spirit and that therefore we must worship Him in spirit, thus indicating that only in the spirit can we serve Him. And John 3 informs us that "that which is born of the flesh is flesh" and "that which is born of the Spirit is spirit." Flesh and spirit are therefore totally different the one from the other. Hence, flesh cannot serve God who is Spirit. Only man's born-again spirit which is born of the Holy Spirit may serve God. So, if one does not have new life in a born-again spirit, he cannot please God even though he may live quite well, for he is still without spirit. This means that the conduct of those who have the Holy Spirit is different in quality from those who do not have a renewed or born-again spirit. These two sets of people may even engage in the same kinds of action, yet the qualities of their actions will be different the one from the other, since each set of people belongs to a different status of life—one being expressive of the flesh and the other being expressive of the spirit. This difference in quality can be likened to a monkey's actions and those of a man. The monkey may appear to do man's work with great similarity, but it does not have man's life. So their qualities of life are quite different.

Let us use another example. Some kinds of materials have the quality of conducting electricity, but some others do not. For instance, wood and rubber are *non-conductors* whereas copper wire is a *conductor.* So the issue here is not a question of whether the quality of the material is good or bad but only a question of whether the material has the quality of conductivity. Accordingly, a person who uses his mind to communicate with God cannot get through to God's Spirit because he is using a non-conductor—the mind. Only by using the conductor which God has established—the spirit of man—can a person get through to God who is Spirit.

Only by using our spirit in serving God and engaging in spiritual activities may we get through to God's Spirit. Should we be numbered among those who are mental, self-willed or emotional people, we are "non-conductors" so far as getting through to God is concerned. In order to be able to fellowship with God, we must first be born again. I must emphatically stress here again that this is not a matter of whether the quality is good or the quantity is sufficient, rather, it is due to a difference in quality. A thick and strong rubber rope, for example, cannot conduct electricity, but small copper circles may do so with no difficulty. Therefore, in this matter of serving God we must be clear that only spirit may contact God who is himself Spirit. Even when we Christians are in fellowship with each other, we need to use our spirit. Christians who use their spirit will gladly respond to all which comes forth from the spirit of other Christians, whether that be word or prayer or action.

At the time of new birth we receive from God a new feeling or spiritual sense enabling us to communicate with God and serve Him. Consequently, new birth is not only relevant to our salvation but is also related to our ability of communicating with and serving God. This is a basic Christian truth. In spiritual matters, as soon as a Christian begins and then continues to use his spirit, every question or problem is solved. Before a person believed in the Lord he or she had a thousand questions. But once the person believed, these many questions need no longer be asked or answered, for the believer has now touched the spirit, and consequently all questions are resolved.

The kingdom of God is intimately related to the Holy Spirit, for Romans 14:17 declares that "the kingdom of God is not eating and drinking, but righteousness and peace and joy in the Holy Spirit." You may learn to preach and pray as though being a spiritual person, but all who have well exercised their spirit know what kind of person you really are. Only by using our spirit may we please and serve God in the newness of spirit.[*]

[*] Note: Message given on 8 March 1950.

CHAPTER TWELVE
SPIRITUAL QUALITY (CONCL'D)

"And it came to pass, when the days were well-nigh come that he should be received up, he stedfastly set his face to go to Jerusalem, and sent messengers before his face: and they went, and entered into a village of the Samaritans, to make ready for him. And they did not receive him, because his face was as though he was going to Jerusalem. And when his disciples James and John saw this, they said, Lord, wilt thou that we bid fire to come down from heaven, and consume them as Elijah did? But he turned, and rebuked them and said, Ye know not what manner of spirit ye are of. For the Son of man came not to destroy men's lives but to save them. And they went to another village" (Luke 9:51-56 mgn).

Intention and Spirit

A few Bible translators have considered the word spirit in Luke 9:55 to be the word heart or have even replaced the word spirit with the word manner—"what kind of manner ye are of"—thus indicating that the manner of these two disciples needed to be corrected. Actually the words spirit and manner convey quite different meanings.

One's manner flows out from one's intention. How, then, do we distinguish between spirit and intention? An unsaved person most certainly has intention, but he has no renewed or born-again spirit. A believer, on the other hand, has both renewed spirit and intention. The spirit of a soulish believer may easily be affected by his intention. I have already pointed out that a man's spirit has no quality of its own. It may take a young person thirty years of being a good Christian to recognize the fact that his spirit has no quality. The longer one lives out the Christian life the more that believer recognizes the fact that one's spirit in and of itself has no quality. The development and growth of quality in the Christian's spirit is derived or emanates from that believer's self or soul. Just as pure water in and of itself has no quality so the spirit has none either. When different things are added to the water, those things give qualities to the water. If, for example, soy sauce is added to the water, such additive gives water the quality of soy sauce.

Similarly is it with the human spirit. The spirit given by God to us is the same to everybody. But because men are different in their selves or souls, their spiritual qualities will turn out to be different as well. And further, because the intention of our soul-life may at times be unclean, therefore, our spirit will at times come forth unclean as well. Our intention is, among other things, what we think of our future and what we plan of our business. These will attach themselves to our spirit, thus giving our spirit a series of various qualities. Why did the Lord Jesus say to His two disciples that their spirit was wrong? Simply because the spirit of the disciples differed from His own, for the Lord's spiritual attitude towards the world was then, and still is, that no one should die from his or her sin, since as He himself said: "the Son of man came not to destroy ... lives but to save them."

The world is a strange place. No one in the world will ever compassionately consider the life of others as did Christ. For the intention of man is selfish in character. For instance, suppose you failed to emerge at the top of your class in your school examination. And suppose, further, that the number-one student becomes sick and is sent to the hospital for an operation. You in your selfishness hope he will die! Must anyone die because he is wiser than you are? This kind of selfish intention is even more evident in the realm of politics. If one fails to climb to the top, he turns to hoping that his political enemy will be disgraced or soon die. Then, too, as people compete in business, one person will hope that a competing manager will die so that he might advance to that position. Like these various worldly examples of selfish intention, the spirit of Jesus' two disciples was wrong, for their intention was that of hatred instead of mercy. Hence, the Lord denied their request, for His spirit did not entertain the thought in the least that anyone should die. That is why, in His censure of these Sons of Thunder, Jesus declared that the Son of man came to *save* life, not to destroy it. Such was the Lord's soulical intention here, and thus was it the quality of His spirit as well.

The intention of Jesus' two disciples was wrong and their spirit was therefore wrong as well. But unbelievers have only intention void of spirit. Their intention is hidden within and not expressed directly. But the spirit of the saved person may launch out, followed by that one's intention. With respect to an unbeliever, the keen observer may know this unbeliever's intention within through the words he speaks. But with respect to a Christian, there is actually something of both intention and spirit coming forth from within. All who have habitually exercised their spirits will recognize and detect this. Whereas the intention of an unsaved person remains hidden within, the intention of a Christian comes forth with his spirit. As the spirit of one Christian comes forth and touches the spirit of a second Christian, the latter is conscious of something coming forth from the first Christian. An unbeliever may deceive others with his words regarding his hidden intention within; but when a Christian's spirit comes forth, the believer cannot hide it from those who have learned before God in their spirits.

How to Have A Right Spirit

How can we have a right spirit? The coming forth of the spirit of a person brings out the flavor of that person's soul- or self-life, and thus it becomes the flavor or taste of that person's personality. Therefore, for one's spirit to be right, one needs for his or her soul-life to be dealt with, since what a person's quality is in that one's outward man—the soul—will be the quality of that person's spirit.

At the time of new birth God gives to every believer a new spirit with no quality therein, its quality having to come from elsewhere—from his dealt-with soul. If a Christian has less spiritual learning before God and less soul-dealing at His hands, his personal spirit will to that degree be incorrect or wrong.

It is relatively easy for a believer with a good memory to quickly learn and/or adopt the patterns of a given preacher's teaching as well as his vocabulary and his tone, the borrowing believer thus thinking that his mastery of such materials will bestow upon him a right spirit. However, in attempting to adopt into one's spirit the substance and style of preaching of another Christian, the endeavor will prove ineffective: it just does not "click." Yes, you may have the teaching, words and tone of someone else, but the condition of your spirit remains the same—there not being any progress or purification taking place. If a believer does not have a pure spirit, he is not suitable for ministering the gospel message from an impure spirit. Otherwise, it would be like trying to deliver another's message with that other person's spirit.

The Lord has recently given me a burden, and that is, to observe if a young worker—after considerable preparation and on-the-job training—is ready to come forth and work more substantially for the Lord. Many brothers and sisters think that to determine if a young worker is ready to do God's work they need only to listen and observe whether or not the message he gives has the correct doctrine. But in my view, listening to his message occupies merely one-tenth of my attention. My attention focused on his spirit occupies nine-tenths of my observation. A person can speak most logically and accurately in terms of doctrine, truth and grammar, yet he may have a rebellious spirit, a rude spirit, a fault-finding spirit, a hostile spirit, a proud spirit, or a hard spirit. His outward words can be soft, pleasant and most engaging, but his inside may be hard as stone.

The unbelievers may have pride but they lack a proud spirit since their spirit is dead. But a Christian may have a proud spirit as well as a prideful heart. So as his words come forth, his spirit is exposed. If a Christian has a bad intention, his spirit will come forth with a quality of badness. A young worker-in-the-making may pray about brokenness, may talk about brokenness, and even preach a message on brokenness, yet he himself has never been broken or broken enough. It is possible for such a believer to cheat himself, but it is not easy to cheat and fool the church and God. For by his spirit the church may know what his soulish intention is.

A Christian's spirit is where God dwells and works, and thus His work can be traced there in that person's spirit. Once a brother wrote a letter to me, saying in part that "brothers and sisters say I am wrong. You too say I am wrong. So, everybody is right, I am always wrong. Since you too say I am wrong, so I must be wrong." Such words conveyed the fact of a hard spirit. After I read the letter, I replied as follows: "It appears that the more you are dealt with, the harder you become. The more you are dealt with, the more rebellious you have become. Even if your word and conduct are right, your spirit is still not right." Let me add here that a person cannot substitute good thought, action and feeling for the lack of developing good qualities of the spirit. I am happy to report that after a few months had gone by I happened to meet this brother and I discerned that his spirit had changed for the better. His teaching had not improved but the quality of his spirit had been raised higher.

We all have the same opportunity to exercise our spirit; hence, do not say that because another brother's wisdom, eloquence, soul power and gift are better than yours, therefore the opportunity for exercising his spirit is better than yours. Not so. God arranges environment, circumstances and events for everyone individually for the purpose of each believer having personal dealings of self, thus enabling each person's spirit to acquire various commendable qualities. We thus need more of the discipline of the Holy Spirit upon our outward man.

Here, then, I would like for us to consider further the discipline of the Holy Spirit. He not only dwells within us to be our life, He also arranges our environment for us to learn. He knows best what kind of environment is best for each of us. There is no environment coming upon us without it having been arranged by the Holy Spirit. The unbelievers may look upon their circumstances of life in terms of chance, accident, happenstance or fate, but not so with Christians. The Lord Jesus told us that even every hair of our head has been numbered by our heavenly

Father (Matthew 10:30). He also indicated that the birds are so cheap that if a person buys four, he would be given another one free (cf. Matthew 10:29a with Luke 12:6a); yet Jesus further said that without the Father's permission not even a single bird would fall to the ground (Matthew 10:29b); how much more valuable are we, Jesus went on to say, than many birds (Matthew 10:31).

Hence, all which happens to us is not a matter of chance or fate but is a set of arrangements provided by God the Creator. And His purpose in all of it is to build us up. The discipline of the Holy Spirit is thus a daily dealing in order to break the hold upon us of our soul-life, resulting in our spiritual quality becoming better and purer. If we want to live a comfortable life and escape from the environment as arranged by the Holy Spirit, our spiritual quality will not be enriched and made purer, though admittedly our hardships will be less in number and severity.

A Christian's spiritual poverty is not caused by his or her birth; rather, it is due to an unwillingness to allow the Lord to work. If, however, we are willing to submit ourselves to the Spirit's discipline as ordained by God, our spirit will become stronger and purer.

There may be those who have been Christians for twenty or thirty years or may have led revival meetings for twenty years, and yet, they may not be those who arouse my attention. For they may be those in whose life I cannot touch a spirit of good quality. If, however, a person's spirit is good, then as soon as I encounter such a one it gives me a soothing sense of anointing. Whatever a person learns in relation to one's soul-life before God is all stored in one's spirit. Such dealing cannot be pretended, for the more a person pretends, the more it will be exposed as being false. I must acknowledge here that some Christians tend to appear spiritual before me in order to obtain my praise. In Shanghai there was a sister who said that brother Nee never praises anyone because no one matches his standard. Actually, the only one who qualifies as the one who has the right to praise others is the Lord Jesus. Those who are spiritual will be loved, praised and rewarded by Him.

Suppose your spirit is bad; nevertheless, I like you and praise you; what good does that accomplish? Or suppose someone hates you in his heart and yet praises you to your face and further says with his mouth that he loves you. He declares with his mouth that he loves you, yet the spirit which comes forth with his words is one of hatred. If you are well learned spiritually before God, you will know and recognize the pretense at once. One may pretend to cheat and fool others, but your spirit cannot be hindered from sensing and detecting that person's insincerity.

There be many whose words are correct and ideas are right and yet their spirits are wrong. The quality of your spirit depends on whether and how you accept the discipline of the Holy Spirit. As you are being dealt with by Him in your self-life you will condemn sin even as the indwelling Spirit has done. If you receive the discipline of the Holy Spirit daily and learn to deal with yourself daily, you will make great spiritual progress. Whether you make progress or not, you yourself may not know but other people will know. In Shanghai people frequently knock at my door, asking to speak with me. As soon as they see me, they ask: "Brother Nee, has my spirit made progress?" Those who so ask are usually those whom I have sensed in my spirit have not made any progress.

Whether or not you have made progress may not be known by you, but other people will know how your spirit is. You yourself do not need to know; in fact, it is better if you do not know. Recall how, whenever Moses came out from before the Lord's presence, his face shone most bright! Yet, though he himself did not know this, the children of Israel knew (Exodus 34:29-30). If while growing up we should look often in the mirror, we could immediately detect any change today from yesterday or sense we have grown physically. But in spiritual matters we should never try to reason things out with our mind. We only need to learn more in our spirit and allow the Holy Spirit to discipline us in our self-life daily.

The Usefulness of Good Spiritual Quality

What is the use of having good spiritual quality? Should the spirits of all the brothers and sisters be clear and high, then they will be able to supply one another in mutual spiritual ministry and the church will be greatly enriched.

I believed in the Lord and was born again in late April 1920. Later that same year I met a sister in Christ by the name of Margaret E. Barber. I received much help from her. My help did not necessarily arise from her words. Rather, by merely seeing her face or being with her or simply walking together with her, I felt the supply of the spirit. In the case of someone else, it might be that only after having heard that person speak or preach would you obtain help from his spirit. With Miss Barber, however, you immediately had a sense of being anointed simply by her sitting quietly in the same room with you, for it did not matter whether she did or said anything. Her mere presence was sufficient to provide true spiritual supply. Today, whoever learns more before God has more spiritual supply to offer to others.

To Serve, One Must Use One's Spirit

As we learn to serve in the church we need to exercise our spiritual sense more and more. We must be in touch with our spirit often, otherwise, we deceive ourselves when engaging in so-called service to God. In genuinely serving God we need to have spiritual reaction from Him. Let us allow our spirit to be moved by Him. We therefore need to have an open spirit before God so as to be able to touch Him as well as be able to touch the spirit of other brothers and sisters. Moreover, let the spirit of other brethren in the church touch you and even move you. No joy or tear or word can necessarily move you; it is only the spirit that can touch you and move you to serve God and others. Hence, any service done for God without using your spirit has no worth before Him.

Now in order for the church to have spiritual service there is a need first for there to be a right spirit among God's people. If my spirit is open and the spirits of the brothers and sisters are open, then together we touch God in the spirit and serve Him in the midst. This, then, will mean that the entire church will be engaged in spiritual service. If, however, you attempt to serve God in the first instance with your mind, will or emotion, my spirit, and that of other brethren, will be shut up. The use of the spirit by all the brothers and sisters is therefore extremely important in the church meetings and in service one towards another. We must learn to follow the spirit in all things.

How do we know if a thing done in the church is right or wrong? It depends on how our spirits react and judge. All judgment and fellowship are to be considered on the basis of spirit, not on the basis of wrong opinions. For example, if, in preaching the gospel, what you speak forth is from your brain, it can only touch others' brains but cannot move or touch or convict the conscience in their dead spirits. In order to touch people's spirits you must not—in the first instance—select or use words out of your brain. We must refuse to accept what our spirit rejects. If we can learn to always reject what the spirit rejects, the quality of our spirit may remain high.

Hereafter, in our evaluation of our young workers-in-training as to what corrections need to be pointed out regarding their preaching or giving testimonies, we should base our decisions on the state or condition of these workers' spirits as to whether there was spiritual supply therein. As I have mentioned several times before, when a man born blind eventually sees, he will henceforth use his eyes to see and cease using his ears and hands as substitutes for his heretofore blind eyes. Similarly, that should be the attitude and practice of our younger workers: they should use their spirits more and their brains less in their service to God. Just as various organs in our body grow stronger from increased usage, so our spirits grow stronger as they are used more.

Next, I wish to say the following to our young people. If your spirit moves more, you should offer up longer prayers. On the other hand, if there is less spiritual sense, then your prayers should be short. Learn to ask an older brother or sister after the prayer meetings. After a number of times like that, you will have learned to know your spirit in this regard, and thus you can pray in the spirit more. Please be advised that short prayers are not necessarily right nor are long prayers necessarily wrong. Whether we open or close our mouths, we sin against the Holy Spirit if we are not under His control.

Finally, let me observe that in our spiritual service together in the church we not only need to be coordinated with one another but we also must have good and strong spiritual quality. May God have mercy on us that we may learn more.*

* Note: Message given on 9 March 1950.

OTHER TITLES AVAILABLE
From Christian Fellowship Publishers

By Watchman Nee

<u>The Basic Lesson Series</u>
Vol. 1 - A Living Sacrifice
Vol. 2 - The Good Confession
Vol. 3 - Assembling Together
Vol. 4 - Not I, But Christ
Vol. 5 - Do All to the Glory of God
Vol. 6 - Love One Another

Aids to "Revelation"
Amazing Grace
Back to the Cross
A Balanced Christian Life
The Better Covenant
The Body of Christ: A Reality
The Character of God's Workman
Christ the Sum of All Spiritual Things
The Church and the Work – 3 Vols
"Come, Lord Jesus"
The Communion of the Holy Spirit
The Finest of the Wheat – Vol. 1
The Finest of the Wheat – Vol. 2
From Faith to Faith
From Glory to Glory
Full of Grace and Truth – Vol. 1
Full of Grace and Truth – Vol. 2
Gleanings in the Fields of Boaz
The Glory of His Life
God's Plan and the Overcomers
God's Work
Gospel Dialogue
Grace for Grace
Heart-to-Heart Talks
Interpreting Matthew
Journeying towards the Spiritual
The King and the Kingdom of Heaven
The Latent Power of the Soul
Let Us Pray
The Life That Wins
The Lord My Portion
The Messenger of the Cross
The Ministry of God's Word
My Spiritual Journey
The Mystery of Creation
Powerful According to God
Practical Issues of This Life
The Prayer Ministry of the Church
The Release of the Spirit
Revive Thy Work
The Salvation of the Soul
The Secret of Christian Living
Serve in Spirit
The Spirit of Judgment
The Spirit of the Gospel
The Spirit of Wisdom and Revelation
Spiritual Authority
Spiritual Discernment
Spiritual Exercise
Spiritual Knowledge
The Spiritual Man
Spiritual Reality or Obsession
Take Heed
The Testimony of God
Whom Shall I Send?
The Word of the Cross
Worship God
Ye Search the Scriptures

OTHER TITLES AVAILABLE
From Christian Fellowship Publishers

By Stephen Kaung

The "God Has Spoken" Series
Seeing Christ in the Old Testament, Part One
Seeing Christ in the Old Testament, Part Two
Seeing Christ in the New Testament

Discipled to Christ
God's Purpose for the Family
The Gymnasium of Christ
In the Footsteps of Christ
New Covenant Living & Ministry
The Songs of Degrees – *Meditations on Fifteen Psalms*
The Splendor of His Ways – *Seeing the Lord's End in Job*